THE TRIAL OF WILLIAM DRENNAN

edited by John Larkin

The Trial of

WILLIAM DRENNAN

on a Trial for Sedition, in the Year 1794

AND

his Intended Defence

EDITED, WITH AN INTRODUCTION, BY

JOHN FRANCIS LARKIN

Reid Professor of Criminal Law
in the University of Dublin

IRISH ACADEMIC PRESS

The text used in this book is reset from the 1794 edition
of the *Full Report* of Drennan's trial,
the title page of which is reproduced on page 35,
and, in the case of the Appendix, from Drennan's
Fugitive pieces, in verse and prose (Belfast, 1815).

Typeset by Seton Music Graphics Ltd, Bantry, Co. Cork, for
Irish Academic Press, Kill Lane, Blackrock, Co. Dublin, Ireland.

British Library Cataloguing in Publication Data
The trial of William Drennan (with an introduction
by John Larkin).
1. Ireland. Seditious libel. Trials, history
344.1505231

ISBN 0-7165-2457-0

Printed in Great Britain by
Billing & Sons Ltd, Worcester

CONTENTS

INTRODUCTION

William Drennan was born on 23 May 1754[1] in the manse of the first Presbyterian congregation in Rosemary Street, Belfast, where his father Thomas Drennan was minister. Of the Revd Thomas Drennan, little is known except what may be inferred from his powerful influence on his son and friendship with the leading men in "new light" Presbyterianism.[2] William Drennan took the degree of AM at the university of Glasgow in 1771 and after graduating MD from the university of Edinburgh in 1778 commenced practice as a physician in Belfast. He removed to Newry in 1783, and to Dublin in 1789.

Although active in the Volunteer movement during the heady years of the Irish constitutional revolution[3] and the author of an acclaimed pamphlet *Letters of Orellana, an Irish Helot*,[4] Drennan's greatest contribution to political development at this period lay in his origination of the United Irish

---

1. The best short biography of Drennan is that found in the introduction to *Glendalloch and other Poems by the Late Dr Drennan*, 2nd ed. (Dublin, 1859). See also the MS notes by F.J. Biggar in Belfast Central Library: Biggar MSS Q237. Much useful information on the Revd Thomas Drennan is to be found in the unpublished Queen's University of Belfast PhD thesis by the Revd Dr JW Nelson "Presbyterianism in Belfast 1642–1830" (1986).
2. See the Intended Defence, *infra*, p. 126. For a short account of the non-subscription controversy see W.T. Latimer, *A History of the Irish Presbyterians*, 2nd ed. (Belfast, 1902), pp. 297–313.
3. For the political background see R.B. McDowell, *Ireland in the Age of Imperialism and Revolution 1760–1801* (Oxford, 1979), pp. 275–92.
4. 1785. Originally published in the *Belfast Newsletter*. Drennan later, in a letter to William Bruce, regretted the title as Orellana had failed in his purpose and committed mass suicide with his companions: PRONI D553/36.

movement.[5] Disillusioned with the Volunteer Movement's failure to secure Catholic Emancipation and Parliamentary Reform he outlined in 1784 and 1785 an "entire scheme for a secret inner circle of dedicated radical reformers . . . six years before the United Irish society was formed".[6] In May 1791 five months before the founding of the first Society of United Irishmen in Belfast Drennan wrote to his brother-in-law Samuel McTier urging the establishment of "A benevolent conspiracy—a plot for the people—no *Whig* club—no party title—the Brotherhood its name—the Rights of Men and the Greatest Happiness of the Greatest Number its end—its general end Real Independence to Ireland, and Republicanism its particular purpose".[7]

After the formation of the Dublin Society of United Irishmen in November 1791 Drennan occupied a central position in the organisation, holding the office of president at intervals throughout 1792 and 1793.[8] Among other things he secured the adoption of the oath that would characterise the entire movement, defending it against the strictures of Tone and Thomas Russell.[9]

5. See the seminal essay by A.T.Q. Stewart, "'A Stable Unseen Power': Dr William Drennan and the origins of the United Irishmen" in Bossy and Jupp (eds), *Essays Presented to Michael Roberts* (Belfast, 1976).
6. Ibid., p. 85.
7. D.A. Chart (ed.), *The Drennan Letters* (Belfast, 1931) (hereafter *Letters*), p. 54.
8. See R.B. McDowell (ed.), *Proceedings of the Dublin Society of United Irishmen* (hereafter *Proceedings*) 17 *Analecta Hibernica* (Dublin, 1949).
9. *Letters*, pp. 65–6. 'I AB in the presence of God do pledge myself to my country, that I will use all my abilities and influence in the attainment of an impartial and adequate representation of the Irish nation in Parliament and as a means of absolute and immediate necessity in accomplishing this chief good of Ireland, I shall do whatever lies in my power to forward a brotherhood of affection, an identity of interests, a communion of rights, and an union of power among Irishmen of all religious persuasions without which every reform must be partial, not national, inadequate to the wants, delusive to the wishes and insufficient for the freedom and happiness of this country.' See also Drennan's debate with Bruce in *Belfast Politics* (Belfast, 1794), pp. 141–67.

The growth of the United Irish movement had by 1792 assumed a form that could not be ignored by government. An announcement of the formation of a "first national battalion" of Volunteers, sporting overtly republican trappings, led government to proscribe a meeting scheduled for 9 December 1792. This did not, according to Drennan, "prevent H. Rowan[10] and one or two other *Protestants* from walking with the green uniform and side arms".[11] A more substantial United Irish challenge to government appeared some days later. That challenge came as an address to the volunteers agreed by the Dublin Society of United Irishmen on 14 December 1792.[12]

What resulted from the address to the volunteers was not a mobilisation of radical opinion throughout the country but the provision to government of a useful pretext for prosecution. By the end of 1794 the address had been the basis for the prosecution not only of Drennan but of Archibald Hamilton Rowan and the proprietors of the radical *Northern Star* newspaper.[13] Rowan was the first to be targeted by government; he was arrested at the end of December 1792 and admitted to bail by Mr Justice Downes.[14] As the author of the address Drennan was conscious of his own liability to prosecution, but during the long wait for Rowan's trial on 29 January 1794 he continued to assure relations in Belfast of his security.[15]

10. Archibald Hamilton Rowan (1751-1834), United Irishman. In exile 1794–1803. Had his outlawry reversed and successfully pleaded the Royal Pardon. See *Autobiography of Archibald Hamilton Rowan* (Dublin, 1840).
11. *Letters*, p. 105.
12. *Proceedings*, p. 47.
13. See *Report of the Trial of Archibald Hamilton Rowan* (Dublin: printed for Archibald Hamilton Rowan, Esquire, and sold by P. Byrne, 1794) and (William Sampson), *A Faithful Report of the second Trial of the Proprietors of the Northern Star* (Belfast, 1795).
14. See *Report of the Trial of Archibald Hamilton Rowan*, pp. 65-6.
15. *Letters*, p. 176.

At this time Drennan's liberty probably depended largely on a former neighbour from Newry. John Pollock, an ambitious and capable attorney, enjoyed a commanding eminence in the control and supply of government intelligence.[16] He had already procured the key crown witness for Rowan's trial[17] and was anxious to increase his knowledge of the United Irish leadership. On 25 November 1792 Drennan wrote in some astonishment to his sister Mrs Martha McTier that he had received a call from Pollock: "our conversation, or rather his turned upon his belief that we were all selling our wares to the best advantage, but in different manners. . . . He concluded with saying,'Drennan, I am your friend, and whenever you wish to befriend yourself and get some good of your abilities, apply to me.'"[18] Although his response to the invitation was negative Drennan continued to permit himself to be socially courted by Pollock until his limited intelligence value led to a switch from charm to veiled menaces, and ultimately to a cessation of friendly contact towards the middle of 1793.[19]

Facing the concrete prospect of a trial for seditious libel since 1792, Rowan waited until 29 January 1794 for it to take place. During that time he resolved to base his defence on a vindication of the address rather "than on any minor object".[20] This was, obviously, of considerable interest to Drennan. He wrote to Samuel McTier in January 1794 describing how he had thought himself

16. I am currently working on the career of this remarkable man who was, *inter alia*, at various times (usually the same time) Deputy Clerk of the Pleas in the Court of Exchequer, Clerk of the Reports in the Court of Chancery, Transcripter and Foreign Apposer in the Court of Exchequer, Crown Solicitor for the Home Circuit and an active JP.
17. See *Report of the Trial of Archibald Hamilton Rowan*, p. 24
18. *Letters*, pp. 96–7.
19. Ibid., p. 150.
20. Drennan to Samuel McTier, 21 January 1794: *Letters*, p. 182.

called upon to write the following note to [John Philpot] Curran[21] without speaking to Rowan. . . . 'Mr Rowan is, I hear, to be tried . . . for the distribution of an Address to the Volunteers of Ireland. . . . If the paper be not in itself seditious, the distribution of it, I imagine, cannot be seditious, and as the intention with which it was written is the pith of criminality and the ground of decision, who can declare that intention so well as he who wrote it? I wrote it, and were I asked as exculpatory evidence whether I had any design of stirring up revolt or of exciting resistance to existing laws, I could answer No, before God and my country, No. My single design was to endeavour to revive the Volunteer Army of Ireland, and I wrote as if I had felt the departed spirit of 30,000 of my countrymen stirring in my breast. . . . I do not think I could read a lecture more exhortatory to peace and tranquillity than this very paper, and if the jury do find it a malicious, scandalous and seditious libel, the public may suspect they are wrong, but I *know* it'.[22]

A pooterish aspect of Drennan is disclosed by his finding it "odd" that Curran made no reply to this bizarre communication.

No benefit to Rowan could have flowed from Drennan's offer. In the criminal law of the late eighteenth century the statement "that the very essence and pith of all criminality consists in the intention"[23] was of very limited application to seditious libel.[24] Curran faced an already difficult task on

21. See infra, p. 16.
22. *Letters*, p. 183.
23. *Infra*, pp. 123–4.
24. And indeed generally in the criminal law of the period. As the accused could not give evidence on oath, "intention must be judged by the circumstances of the fact": Hale, *History of the Pleas of the Crown*, Wilson's edition (London, 1778) I, p. 508–9. This lead to intention being presumed. Drennan in any event is probably confusing intention with motive.

11

Rowan's instructions without handling Drennan's legally irrelevant and largely self-justifying intervention. Even without this, Curran did not enjoy Drennan's good opinion. As a spectator of a trial in Dundalk in 1785 Drennan found him "the fiercest imp of the pandemonium"[25], nor were Curran's idiosyncratic politics any more to his taste. After Drennan's acquittal Curran seems to have cultivated him assiduously; he acknowledged Drennan's thanks in a note that expressed admiration for his virtues and talents, dined with him, and returned the fee that Drennan could ill afford to pay.[26] Despite this Curran remained "a genius & a blackguard",[27] with his famed wit merely "a sort of wanton malignity"[28]. Although Drennan ruefully acknowledged that this was a "pretty return"[29] for Curran's defence and generosity, he remained incapable of more favourable assessment.

Curran's conduct of Rowan's defence, although circumscribed at his client's insistence, has furnished what has been deservedly considered one of the classics of Irish forensic oratory.[30] This did not prevent Rowan's conviction and a sentence of two years imprisonment, a fine of £500 and being bound in the sum of £2000, with two sureties of £1000, to keep the peace and be of good behaviour for seven years.[31] The maximum punishment for a misdemeanour[32] such as seditious libel was an unlimited period of imprisonment and/or fine, so that, severe though Rowan's punishment was, it could not be legally impeached.

25. *Letters*, p. 32
26. PRONI Drennan Letters D591/580
27. PRONI Drennan Letters D591/523 Drennan to Samuel McTier 2 August 1794.
28. PRONI Drennan Letters D591/530 Drennan to Martha McTier 14 October 1794.
29. Ibid.
30. See Charles Phillips, *Recollections of Curran and Some of His Contemporaries* (London and Dublin, 1818), p. 185
31. See *Report of the Trial of Archibald Hamilton Rowan* p. 152.
32. At common law crimes were (and in theory at least still are in Ireland) divided into three classes: treason, felonies, and misdemeanours.

Drennan complained of the injustice of Rowan's treatment: "A jury find a man guilty and three men sitting on a bench under the influence of the Crown, can, constitutionally and legally, adjudge any fine from one pound to several thousands, any imprisonment from a month to seven years, and for aught I know, to a lifetime. Will all the visionary theories of checks and counterchecks show that there is no injustice in this?"[33]

Mingled with his scorn for the frailties of the constitution is a personal fear of ruin. This increased with news that Pollock's intelligence-gathering operations were now directed particularly against him.[34] An effort was being made to trace the actual author of the address and inquiries were made at the house of the printer of the *National Evening Star*. This was too much for the fiery Martha McTier, who wrote to Pollock upbraiding him for his pursuit of her brother: "cease, 'tis a damning cause, nor can it come to good".[35] Pollock's reply was a masterpiece of vulpine elegance:

Not having as I think the honour of being personally known to you, and never having had to my knowledge the favour of your acquaintance, I confess I felt not a little surprise on reading a letter that the post brought me this day with your name signed to it. It is a composition, no doubt, of great excellence and imagination, but as I have not yet submitted to the modern operation of being fraternized against my will, I should have declined answering it were it not that it bears the name of a gentlewoman subscribed to it. . . . As to the advice

A felony on conviction occasioned at common law forfeiture of lands and goods and usually capital punishment. A misdemeanour was punishable at common law only with fine and/or imprisonment. See Edmund Hayes *A Digest of the Criminal Statute Law of Ireland* second edition (Dublin, 1843), p. 280 and p. 559.

33. *Letters*, p. 187.
34. Ibid., pp. 187–90.
35. Ibid., p. 191.

you have done me the honour to give me, I receive it with all due consideration. It is peculiarly kind in a lady to whom I have the misfortune of being wholly unknown, to take so much trouble on my account, yet looking up as I do, to the great and superior talent, to the gentleness, the feminine expression, and to the beautiful and amiable insinuation and manners that mark every line of the performance you have bestowed upon me, allow me to assure you, that whenever I shall venture to solicit your advice I shall most thankfully receive and attend to it. . . . [36]

If Drennan cannot have been reassured by the result of his sister's intemperate correspondence, the latter was further alarmed when she heard of Rowan's escape from Newgate on 1 May. She speculated nervously about who the government would fix upon to fill "the late vacated seat at Newgate"[37] and warned Drennan against a romanticisation of political captivity. By this time any warning came too late. At a quarter to eight in the evening of 12 May 1794 Drennan was arrested on a charge of seditious libel and spent the night in Newgate.[38] Professing no unease at the arrest, he took the opportunity of putting Pollock to the embarrassment of refusing to become a surety on his behalf,[39] and gave every appearance of firmness at the prospect of trial.

In the midst of discussions with and about lawyers Drennan floated his own ideas on the conduct of his case. Conceding that the Address to the Volunteers had been "prejudged", he

36. Ibid., p. 192.
37. Ibid., p. 195.
38. See J.T. Gilbert, *A History of the City of Dublin* (Dublin, 1854), I, p. 274. Situated in Green St the "new" Newgate was opened in 1780 to serve as the main Dublin prison. There is a fine description of Newgate in the early nineteenth century in G.N. Wright, *An Historical Guide to the City of Dublin*, second edition (London, 1825), pp. 111–2.
39. *Letters*, p. 201.

proposed to rest his defence "by giving a *set-off* in a sincere, simple, succinct account of the *context* of my life and political conduct which, by comparison with one act, the subject of accusation, may counterbalance in the minds of the jury, and operate by way of mitigation, on the *discretion* of the court".[40] A great deal of time was spent on this "set-off" but it was only shortly before the trial that Drennan was told that he would not have the opportunity to present it to a jury, although he might, if convicted, offer it in mitigation of sentence.[41] Seventeen years later Drennan published it as an "Intended defence on a trial of sedition in the year 1794"; as political rhetoric it is magnificent (see Appendix); as a plea in mitigation one can only shudder at its likely results.

For legal advice Drennan turned naturally to the lawyers in the Dublin Society of United Irishmen, particularly Thomas Addis Emmet and Simon Butler. That the Society was well stocked with lawyers was quickly remarked upon, and it is curious that the principal witness against Drennan, William Paulet Carey, should disparage them not only in a celebrated pamphlet[42] but during the course of his testimony also. From a list of 200 members of the Society, constructed by Dr R.B. McDowell, it appears that 30 attorneys and 26 barristers had been admitted,[43] and even if there is some truth in Carey's reference to "two or three persons of profession, who wished for practice and had it not",[44] it is clear that the Society had several lawyers of ability and substance among its members.[45] Drennan had intended initially to retain only counsel connected with the Society to ensure that his stance was not

40. Ibid., p. 204.
41. Ibid., p. 206.
42. *An Appeal to the People of Ireland* (Dublin, 1794).
43. R.B. McDowell, *The Personnel of the Dublin Society of United Irishmen, 1791–4* (1940) 2 IHS 12 at 15.
44. Infra, p. 69.
45. Apart from Butler, Dowling and Emmet, William Sampson and William Ridgeway may be mentioned.

compromised by a reliance on a merely technical defence. Soon, coming under pressure from lawyers within the Society, he agreed to retain Curran to lead his defence and, unlike Rowan, let nothing hinder the fight for acquittal.[46]

As first settled Drennan's legal team consisted of Curran, Butler and Emmet instructed by Matthew Dowling, attorney. Curran (1750–1817) was much more than a popular orator. It is unfortunate that his technical ability as a lawyer and the due measure of his statesmanship are obscured partly by the distorting praise of the nineteenth century, partly by the paucity of materials for an assessment of his career as Master of the Rolls in Ireland (1806–14) but also by his own penchant for buffoonery, assisted (if that is the proper word) by the distinctly simian cast of his features.[47] Called to the Irish bar in 1775, he took silk and was elected to parliament in 1783. In 1794 he was at the height of his powers and at the head of the profession. Butler (1757–97) was the third son of Lord Mountgarret and the first president of the United Irish society of Dublin. He was called to the Irish bar in 1778[48] and took silk in 1784. In March 1793 Butler had been imprisoned for contempt of parliament and on his release later that year found himself subject to increasing financial embarrassment. On Monday 23 June 1794 Drennan wrote ruefully to Martha McTier that Butler was unwilling to leave his house except on Sundays[49] for fear of arrest on civil process and felt unable to act as counsel.[50] Butler's circumstances did

46. *Letters* p. 205.
47. See F. Elrington Ball, *The Judges in Ireland, 1221–1921* (London, 1926) (hereafter *Ball*), II pp. 337–8. The King's Inns portrait of Curran in his judicial robes is a masterpiece of flattery.
48. See *King's Inns Admission Papers 1607–1867* (Dublin, 1982), p. 67. There is a DNB entry for Butler.
49. PRONI Drennan Letters D591/503. This letter is incompletely transcribed in *Letters*, p. 206.
50. Sunday being *dies non juridicus* arrest was not possible save for treason, felony or breach of the peace: see Blackstone, *Commentaries on the Laws of England*, (Oxford, 1768), III, p. 290.

not improve; in October 1794 Drennan noted that a bailiff had been watching his furniture and he had left Ireland to defeat his creditors.[51]

Replacing Butler proved difficult. Henry Duquery[52] was initially suggested but between June 23 and 25 William Fletcher (1750–1823) was retained.[53] Beginning his professional life as a doctor of medicine Fletcher quickly moved to law, being called to the Irish bar in 1778. Although never overtly sympathetic to the United Irish movement Fletcher retained an idiosyncratic radicalism even after his appointment as justice of the Irish Court of Common Pleas in 1806. Echoing Curran's 1789 excoriation of the "midnight Adonises"[54] of the Dublin police, Fletcher in a charge to the County Wexford grand jury in 1814 condemned the criminal justice policy of the Irish government and narrowly avoided becoming a casualty of the resulting political storm.[55]

Of all his legal advisers Drennan had the closest relationship with Thomas Addis Emmet[56] (1764–1827). Like Fletcher, Emmet began his career as a doctor. He was called to the Irish bar in 1790, and, as an early member of the Dublin Society of United Irishmen, quickly gained a reputation in cases involving the society. Emmet remained a member of the United Irish movement throughout the period of its increased militarisation in the mid 1790s and was imprisoned

51. PRONI Drennan Letters D591/530.
52. PRONI Drennan Letters D591/503.
53. See *Ball*, p. 338.
54. For a discussion of the controversy over the 'Dublin Police Experiment' see Stanley H. Palmer, *Police and Protest in England and Ireland 1780–1850* (Cambridge, 1988), pp. 119–33. Curran's vivid phrase is to be found in his 1789 speech supporting resolutions criticising waste and patronage in the Dublin police. See Thomas Davis (ed.), *The Speeches of the Right Honorable John Philpot Curran* third edition (Dublin, 1862), pp. 94–6.
55. See Norman Gash, *Mr Secretary Peel* (London, 1985), pp. 182–3.
56. See R.R. Madden, *The United Irishmen their Lives and Times*, third series, second edition (London, 1860).

from 1798 to 1802. On his release he moved to the United States where he enjoyed considerable success as an advocate.[58] Drennan's attorney Matthew Dowling[59] (c.1755–1804) was a prominent early member of the Dublin Society of United Irishmen who was later imprisoned along with Emmet and other important members of the society.

Presenting the case for the crown was a strong group of advocates headed by the Attorney General Arthur Wolfe[60] (1739–1803). Called to the Irish bar in 1766, Wolfe was appointed Solicitor General in 1787 and Attorney General in 1789.

Unimpressed by Wolfe's abilities Drennan thought him "really miserable in his office of public accuser" but grudgingly admitted that he was "accounted a first lawyer."[61] In 1798 Wolfe was appointed Chief Justice of the Court of King's Bench and in his brief tenure of that office gave ample demonstration of his legal learning and sense of justice.[62] Wolfe was assisted by the next senior law officer, Solicitor General, John Toler[63] (1739–1831). Here it is difficult to improve on Ball's summary: "Inherently he was a jovial fox-hunting Tipperary gentleman, with strong protestant and tory predilections."[64] Toler had been called to the Irish bar in 1770, held the office of Solicitor General from 1789 to 1798, and was then Attorney General until he crowned his essentially ignoble career by elevation to Chief Justice of the Court of Common Pleas in 1800.

57. Ibid., pp. 35–43.
58. Ibid., pp. 141–155.
59. See *King's Inns Admission Papers 1607–1867* (Dublin, 1982), p. 141. Dowling was with Emmet exiled under the terms of the Banishment Act 1798 (38 Geo III c.78).
60. See *Ball*, p. 230.
61. *Letters*, p. 184.
62. Most famous is perhaps his conduct in the habeas corpus application by Tone's father: see W.T.W Tone (ed.), *Life of Theobald Wolfe Tone* (Washington, 1826), II, pp. 534–5.
63. See *Ball*, pp. 331–2.
64. Ibid., p. 237.

Although the office of Prime Serjeant had formal precedence over those of Attorney and Solicitor General political reality in 1794 ensured the greater importance of the latter posts.[65] Nevertheless Prime Serjeant James Fitzgerald[66] (1742–1835) enjoyed considerable legal and political standing. Fitzgerald was called to the Irish bar in 1769 and held the office of Prime Serjeant from 1787 to 1799 when his patent was revoked as a response to his opposition to the Union. Of the other crown counsel, Frankland[67] and Ruxton[68] relatively little is known .

Unlike England at this period Ireland experienced substantial central government participation in prosecutions.[69] In 1715 an allowance of £100 was placed on the Irish civil list "for prosecuting criminals."[70] In subsequent years this allowance was given under the heading of solicitor in criminal causes. By 1794 Thomas Kemmis held this office which became something of a Kemmis family monopoly for most of the nineteenth century.[71]

The Irish judges of the revolutionary era have not enjoyed a reputation for the virtues properly associated with their order. Yet any consideration of the background of the mem-

68. This anomaly was rectified by the abolition of the office in 1805. From that date the First Serjeant had precedence only over the Second Serjeant.
66. See *King's Inns Admission Papers 1607–1867* (Dublin, 1982) p. 165; *Alumni Dublinenses* (Dublin, 1935), p. 284. There is a DNB entry for Fitzgerald.
67. See *King's Inns Admission Papers 1607–1867* (Dublin, 1982) p. 176; *Alumni Dublinenses* (Dublin, 1935), p. 305.
68. See *King's Inns Admission Papers 1607–1867* (Dublin, 1982) p. 432; *Alumni Dublinenses* (Dublin, 1935), p. 723.
69. See John McEldowney, "Crown Prosecutions in Nineteenth-Century Ireland" in Hay and Snyder (eds), *Policing and Prosecution in Britain 1750–1850* (Oxford, 1989), pp. 427–57.
70. See 13th Appendix to the *Report of the Select Committee on Civil Government Charges* (1831) IV Parliamentary Papers, p. 410.
71. See McEldowney, *op. cit.*, p. 437 n62. William Kemmis's name is given incorrectly in the footnote.

bers of the Irish Court of King's Bench in 1794 makes it difficult to withhold admiration for their conduct in the trial of a man committed, apparently, to the overthrow of that establishment of which they were the servants. Presiding over the Court of King's Bench was the Chief Justice Lord Clonmell[72] (1739–98) a man whose obsessive pursuit of success appears in his extraordinary diary.[73] In this, along with his worries about flatulence and rivals for preferment, is revealed a demonic appetite for the hard work which, he perceives, is his sole route to the rewards of office and professional acclaim. These were not slow in coming to him; called to the Irish bar in 1765 he became counsel to the Revenue Commissioners in 1772, Solicitor General in 1774, and Attorney General in 1777. His career experienced a partial and temporary setback in 1782 when he was removed from the office of Attorney General to make way for the "patriot" Barry Yelverton. It quickly recovered in 1783 when he picked up the highly lucrative office of Clerk of the Pleas in the Court of Exchequer[74] and was crowned by his appointment as Chief Justice in 1784.

Clonmell entertained no mean opinion of his impartiality; delivering a warning to Patrick Byrne, the publisher of Rowan's trial, he boasted that Rowan "would not have been better used by me, standing in the situation he did, if he was one of the princes of the blood."[75] Although Drennan cannot

72. See *Ball*, p. 222.
73. This was inexplicably printed by his descendants and is in the TCD library. Extracts were published by W.J. Fitzpatrick in *Ireland before the Union* (Dublin, 1867).
74. S.3 of the Irish statute 21 & 22 Geo III c. 18 effected a considerable reform of the procedure on the common law side of the Court of Exchequer with the result that the business of this court was very greatly increased to the profit of its officials and judges. Some exaggerated comments on the value of the office are found in a letter from Drennan to Samuel McTier, PRONI D591/461.
75. See *Autobiography of Archibald Hamilton Rowan* (Dublin, 1840), p. 209.

have shared this view, after his own trial he accepted that "the charge of the judges, Clonmell, Downes and Chamberlaine [*sic*], was on the whole impartial."[76]

Although the three Irish common law courts had an increase of one judge each in 1784[77] only three judges sat at Drennan's trial. The report discreetly records (*infra,* page 44) that Mr Justice Boyd "having been taken ill did not preside" but Drennan's reference to "drunken Boyd"[78] probably contains a shrewder explanation of that judge's non appearance. Of the two puisne judges who sat with Clonmell, one William Downes[79] (1751–1826) became Chief Justice of the King's Bench in succession to Arthur Wolfe in 1803, the other William Tankerville Chamberlain[80] (1751–1802) had been appointed a puisne judge of the Court of Common Pleas in 1793 but transferred to the King's Bench in 1794.

The central figure in Drennan's trial is not, of course, Drennan, who as the accused was an incompetent witness at common law[81] but the principal crown witness, William Paulet Carey[82] (1759–1839). Carey's role in the United Irish movement has already been noted above, but not the least bizarre feature of his career is his abandonment of politics for art dealing and criticism, a transformation so complete that his biographer can only record unhelpfully "[H]e is said to have been a United Irishman."[83]

76. *Letters*, p. 208.
77. *Ball*, pp. 167-8.
78. PRONI Drennan Letters D591/464.
79. See Ball, p. 227.
80. Ibid.
81. A position not altered by statute until 1923 in Northern Ireland and 1924 in Ireland. See Claire Jackson, "Irish Political Opposition to the Passage of Criminal Evidence Reform at Westminster, 1883–98" in McEldowney and O'Higgins (eds), *The Common Law Tradition* (Dublin, 1990), pp. 185-201.
82. The best account of Carey's intriguing career is in Brian Inglis, *The Freedom of the Press in Ireland 1784–1841* (London, 1954), pp. 64–8.
83. DNB, volume 3, p. 987.

As the publisher of *The Rights of Irishmen or National Evening Star* Carey was threatened with prosecution in November 1792 for an item lifted from the *Northern Star* describing the Belfast rejoicing over the French victory at Valmy.[84] On 23 November the Society agreed to support him.[85] More serious, however, was the danger from the government response to the publication of the Address to the Volunteers in the *National Evening Star* of 20 December 1792. On 29 March 1793, after having been arrested and bailed on charges arising out of the latter publication, Carey approached the Society for help again.[86] It was not a good time to ask; the Society was overstretched financially and Carey personally had never been popular, but it would have been difficult for the Society to have shirked a defence of one of its principal manifestos.[87] Although Carey renewed his request at a meeting on 5 April the matter dragged on until November when the Society managed to sidestep the claim. On 1 November it was ordered that Carey exculpate himself at the next meeting from the charge of having published matter disparaging the Society in the *Morning Post*.[88] Although he appeared on 8 November Carey refused to admit or disavow authorship; his comparison of the inquisitorial behaviour of the Society on this occasion with the practice of the Secret Committee of the House of Lords, although shrewd, did not endear him to his judges, and he was expelled.[89]

While effective as a measure of cost cutting in the short term, making an enemy of Carey was a serious misjudgment. Government intelligence was quick to note his value but initially Carey simply wanted money, not revenge on the Society. A message was received from Carey at the Society's meeting

84. Infra, p. 63.
85. *Proceedings*, p. 40.
86. Ibid., p. 71.
87. Ibid., p. 110.
88. Ibid., pp. 91–2.
89. Ibid., pp. 92–3.

on 18 April 1794 warning of his intention to place those members who had given him the Address to print at the mercy of Government if £200 were not made available to compensate his bailsmen in the event of him not abiding his trial.[90] The threat was renewed at the 9 May meeting where interestingly Drennan proposed taking it into consideration; the proposal was rejected, and, as Thomas Collins the government informer perceptively suggested, Carey "may be *had* on very easy terms."[91]

Although Collins was congratulating himself on 17 May that he "was right about Carey, I knew and informed you that he could be very easily had,"[92] Carey did not, in fact, propose to undervalue his services. The final deal struck with government included substantial support for a new pro-administration newspaper as well as a handsome cash payment and an annuity.[93] After the verdict of the jury, however, it is perhaps not surprising that government was unenthusiastic about the fulfilment of its obligations, and even with the threat of litigation Carey was able to recover only a fraction of his reward.[94]

Paradoxically for a paid witness Carey was amazingly honest; apart from a desire to underplay the extent of his personal resentment against Drennan his evidence is measured and accurate. A dishonest witness who desired to protect the value of his own testimony would not have been as reticent in direct examination or as candid about the frailty of his memory. The number of leading questions asked by the Prime Serjeant[95] is no indication of forensic incompetence but shows the difficulty experienced by the Crown in eliciting the necessary proofs from Carey.

90. Ibid., p. 123.
91. Ibid., p. 126.
92. Ibid., p. 127.
93. Inglis, op. cit, p. 66.
94. Ibid., p. 68.
95. A leading question is one which suggests or contains its answer.

To bring home the charge of seditious libel against Drennan, the Crown had to prove publication of the seditious material in the manner specified in one or more of the nine counts in the indictment. In a state trial it was unlikely that a technical slip would be found in the indictment, as, for example, a variance between the text of the Address to the Volunteers as printed in the newspapers and as reproduced in the indictment,[96] but it was essential that the evidence adduced match the manner in which the offence was stated to be committed in at least one of the counts.[97]

Given the requirement of exactness in identity and manner, the chains of proof connecting Drennan with the offence began to assume a distinctly shaky appearance during Carey's evidence. Firstly there was a paper called "The Address to the Volunteers" read by Drennan at the Society's meeting of 14 December 1792 at which Carey was present; then there was a direction from Drennan to Carey to publish the Address in the *National Evening Star* not from the manuscript which had been read but from the *Hibernian Journal* or a printed handbill; finally there is Carey's admission that he could not "swear they were copied word for word."[98]

These flaws appeared even before Curran began his cross examination which began with a general assault on Carey's character and memory.[99] After he had been softened up by Curran's opening questions he was pushed to answers that destroyed any prosecution value in his evidence.[100] Once he had accepted that he was uncertain about the precise contents of the Address as read and as published, Carey broke any evidentially compelling link between himself, Drennan and the Address. That part of the Crown case based solely on Carey's

96. Hence the importance of attending to the reading of the alleged libel "with scrupulous accuracy", *infra*, p. 89.
97. See Blackstone, op. cit., IV, pp. 301–3.
98. Infra, p. 60.
99. Infra, pp. 62–5.
100. Infra, pp. 73–4.

evidence could, however, have been rescued by the answer to a question asked by the jury foreman at the end of Curran's cross examination: "Did he [Drennan] at any time make objection to the accuracy of the publication?"[101] Had the almost inevitable negative been given in response to this question it would have removed the most formidable barrier to conviction. Not surprisingly Curran objected energetically to the question as illegal (which it was not) and notwithstanding its defence by the Attorney General it remained unanswered.

One further line of attack remained to the prosecution; it could still attempt to prove publication in the *Hibernian Journal* through its proprietor, Thomas McDonnell.[102] Like Carey, McDonnell faced a prosecution for publishing the Address but unlike him is not believed to have made a secret engagement with government. After a *Nolle Prosequi*, an order by a law officer of the Crown staying criminal proceedings, had been entered, McDonnell gave evidence for the prosecution but in an apparently half-hearted manner. McDonnell had not been present at the meeting when the Address was agreed nor had he been directly asked to print the paper; a copy of an address had simply been left at his house and it had been printed.[103]

Although an official of the Stamp Office,[104] Francis Lestrange, was able to prove receipt of the particular issue of the *Hibernian Journal* containing the Address, the link with Drennan could not be made on McDonnell's evidence alone. The Crown had to rely on Carey's testimony that Drennan had instructed him to lift the Address from the text already in the *Hibernian Journal*.[105] Thus even though Carey's own

101. Infra, p. 76.
102. See Inglis, op. cit., pp. 82–84.
103. Infra, p. 79.
104. An account of this office and its position in the Irish revenue system is in G.E. Howard, *A Treatise of the Exchequer and Revenue of Ireland* (Dublin, 1776), I, pp. 95–7.
105. Infra, p. 59.

evidence about the *National Evening Star* was worthless in terms of proving publication in that paper, it was essential if any link was to be established between Drennan and the *Hibernian Journal*.[106]

Curran argued that the link was not sufficient to permit the Address to be left to the jury. He stressed the absence of direct evidence that Drennan had authorised the text that appeared in the *Hibernian Journal*, but the thrust of his submissions implicitly disclosed that the issue was the weight of the evidence and as such properly within the province of the jury.[107] Once the Address had been read and the Crown evidence completed the defence called three witnesses. Two, Thomas Traynor and William Wooloughan, principally gave evidence of Carey's rage against Drennan and the Society; the third, Thomas Wright, a Dublin surgeon, was called presumably to further muddy the waters about the origin and identity of the Address as published. On cross examination, however, the Solicitor General lured him into a potentially dangerous exchange over the use of the word 'correct' to describe the published text, a danger he averted only by claiming to have been referring to the canons of grammatical and literary excellence.[108]

With all the evidence complete, the Crown could only rely on two counts, the second and eighth. To convict Drennan the jury ought properly to be sure (the modern rubric "beyond reasonable doubt" was not used) that he had published the Address contained in the indictment and that it was a seditious libel. Before 1792 in England and 1793 in Ireland the issue of libel or no libel was a matter exclusively for the court; but after Fox's libel act and its Irish equivalent, the 33 Geo III c.63, the jury was given the determination of the whole issue at trial. As the traverser (the name given to the person

106. McDonnell himself, it will be remembered, did not do this.
107. Infra, pp. 84–5.
108. Infra, p. 96.

26

pleading not guilty to a misdemeanour)[109] Drennan could try to disprove publication or argue that the Address was not libellous. It was not a defence as Lord Clonmell said "that he thought it a good measure"[110]; Drennan knew the contents and did not therefore publish accidentally or unknowingly he had the requisite mens rea for the offence.

In cases of libel this doctrine has shown quite extraordinary powers of endurance. The House of Lords in the 1979 blasphemous libel case of *Lemon*[111] held by a majority that it was not necessary to prove that the accused intended to outrage Christianity, it being sufficient that such would be the probable effect of the words published. This contrasts with the established preference of Irish criminal law for the subjective theory of liability, a theory increasingly favoured also by the English courts. In another context the offence of seditious libel has been oddly topical at the time of writing with the attempt in *Regina* v *Bow Street Magistrates Court, ex parte Choudhary*[112] to apply it to Salman Rushdie's novel, *The Satanic Verses*.

Curran's closing speech, apart from its result, cannot have been entirely pleasing to Drennan. Curran virtually concedes the libellous nature of the Address and concentrates on the flaws in Carey's testimony. Apart from some good jokes at the expense of the Police, Dublin Corporation and the Militia, there is no attempt comprehensively to defend the Address. Nor is there any attempt to make anything of Drennan's character; indeed Curran is at pains to distance himself from his client and devotes a substantial part of his speech to a defence of his own professional integrity rather than Drennan's hitherto blameless existence. There is little truth, therefore, in Drennan's assertion that, although his Intended Defence

109. See Hayes, op. cit. p. 674.
110. Infra, p. 120.
111. [1979] AC 617.
112. *The Independent*, 10 April 1990.

27

was undelivered, it "was communicated in such a way as to contribute to the acquittal which took place."[113]

The Intended Defence is an important contribution to the development of the radical Presbyterian consciousness. In its evocation of the great names of the Northern Non-Subscribers[114] he establishes a legitimacy for the politics of the Northern Dissenters. While one may be sceptical about the reverence a Dublin jury, composed in all probability of members of the Established Church, would have had for the names of John Abernethy,[115] Michael Bruce,[116] Francis Hucheson[117] and James Duchal,[118] the most important feature of this pantheon is that internally it secured Drennan against public attacks on the alien jacobinism of the United Irish Society.

Again the same technique is employed with reference to the classics of English Dissent,[119] the emphasis is on the domestic tradition of liberty of conscience, and any revolutionary implications are firmly exorcised by the ample homage paid to the influence of Locke.[120] Particularly interesting is

113. Infra, p. 142.
114. Interestingly in James Mackay, *A sermon Preached in the Old Meeting House in Belfast, February 28th 1768 on Occasion of the Death of the Late Reverend Mr Thomas Drennan* (Belfast, 1768), p. 28 the same names are given as the friends of Drennan's father.
115. 1680–1740. Minister of Wood Street Congregation, Dublin, 1730–1740.
116. D.1735. Minister of Holywood, County Down, 1711–35. Father of Drennan's early friend William Bruce.
117. 1694–1746. Professor of moral philosophy in the University of Glasgow, 1729–1746. One of the most influential figures in the Scottish Enlightenment.
118. 1697–1761. Succeeded John Abernethy as minister of Wood Street, 1741–61.
119. Significant here is Philip Furneaux who in his *Letters to the Honourable Mr Justice Blackstone* (which received its second Dublin edition in 1771) challenges the use of human law to promote religious truth: "Conviction is always produced by the light which is struck into the mind and never by compulsion or the force of human authority" (p. 20).
120. Infra, p. 130.

the reference to Micaiah Towgood's *The Dissenting Gentle-man's Letters in Answer to Mr White*. Drennan probably used and grew up with the fourth Dublin edition (1766) of this work, an edition prepared by Northern Presbyterian ministers. The importance of the work, however, is best shown in the accretions to the next Irish edition (Newry, 1816) produced by Drennan's friend William Bruce, where the Non-Subscribing Presbytery of Antrim is shown to be seised of the essence of the Reformation principle of private judgment.[121] Obviously Drennan hoped that if these resonances were caught by the jury the injustice of "he is an honest man but reasons of state require his punishment"[122] would be acknowledged in acquittal.

Happily this strategy did not in fact burden the court. The main charge to the jury, that of Lord Clonmell, deals simply with the issues of libel and publication. The jury is invited to take full account of the attacks on the credibility of Carey and to resolve any final indecision in favour of the traverser.[123] Downes's charge is on similar lines, but there is a significant doctrinal addition in Chamberlain's, where there is a specific caution to the jury founded on Carey's character as an *accomplice*.[124] It is an unfortunate truism that the value of and response to the evidence of accomplices is currently a matter of legal and political controversy.[125] During the nineteenth century in Ireland the issue generated a degree of refinement and debate unsurpassed by any other question in the law of evidence[126] but the Judge's charges in this trial

121. Towgood, op. cit. (Newry, 1816), pp. 392-404.
122. Infra, p. 141.
123. Infra, p. 120.
124. Infra, p. 121.
125. See for example: North Belfast Independent Unionist Association, *The Supergrass System—What Saith the Scriptures?* (Belfast, 1985); Concerned Community Organisation Belfast, *In the Government's Arsenal—the Supergrass* (Belfast, 1984); Tony Gifford, *Supergrasses—the Use of Accomplice Evidence in Northern Ireland* (London, 1984).
126. For a breakdown of judicial opinion see Hayes, op. cit., pp. 7–9.

suggest both the relatively recent growth of a separate accomplice evidence doctrine and perhaps the insight that fundamentally the question is one of witness assessment *tout court* and should be left to the jury without elaboration.

A gushing tribute to trial by jury was unlikely to come from Drennan during his ordeal. His major fear seemed to be not judicial partiality but a jury composed of "aristocrats".[127] Certainly the attempt made at the beginning of the trial to challenge Sir John Trail *propter affectum* floundered on the doctrine laid down in William Hawkins's *Treatise of the Pleas of the Crown* that a potential juror could not be asked a question tending to his own disgrace[128] and doubtless added to Drennan's unease. Judicial control of the jury is most vividly evident when it appears after the delivery of the verdict on count two of the indictment that the jury, dismayed by the cheering of the populace, might like to reconsider count eight but are stopped by Downes.[129] Nonetheless, given the antipathy to the Address it is remarkable how closely the jury adhered to the rules, especially when a certain robustness of interpretation would have placed a political opponent at the mercy of the Court.

After the trial Drennan obtained the results of an informal survey of his jurors. He reported to Martha McTier that initially seven—White, Roe, Bibby, Little, Foot, Hamilton, and Alexander—had been in favour of acquittal, with Trail, Lindsay, Woodward, Bloxham, and Galway against.[130] Of the Grand Jury who found the Bill of Indictment[131] against him,

127. *Letters*, p. 208.
128. On the role of the jury generally in Eighteenth Century trials for seditious libel see Thomas Andrew Green *Verdict According to Conscience* (Chicago and London, 1985), pp. 318-55.
129. Infra, p. 121. Here the judge is not identified but Samuel McTier, *Letters*, p. 208 indicates that it was Downes.
130. *Letters*, p. 210.
131. It was a general principle of the common law that no person should be put to trial on any criminal charge unless such charge was sup-

formally beginning the King's Bench stage of his prosecution, Drennan found nothing further to note than his original dismay at the improbable haste with which they found a true bill against him.[132]

Drennan's acquittal was the cause of substantial inconvenience and distress to at least one Dublin citizen, Samuel Gardiner. On the night of the trial when the verdict was announced noisy celebrations disturbed the hall and Court of King's Bench. John Giffard, one of the High Sheriffs of the City of Dublin, arrested one of the most active revellers and on finding it to be Gardiner released him knowing that he would be able to secure the person of this "opulent citizen" at a more convenient time. On 5 July 1794 after the Court had made a conditional order to attach[133] Gardiner for contempt, argument was heard against making the order absolute. In his replying affidavit Gardiner admitted that he had described Giffard as "a rascal and a scoundrel"[134] but only in response to the High Sheriff's unjustified assault. He denied active participation in the disturbance. Delivering judgment on the following day, the three judges sitting (Boyd still presumably indisposed) considered that Gardiner's public abuse of Giffard amounted to a contempt and accordingly made an absolute order for attachment.[135]

During the trial Drennan penned an affecting note to Martha McTier. In explaining the wobbly handwriting he

ported by the oaths of twelve men sitting on a Grand Jury. A Grand Jury composed of at least twelve and not more than twenty three freeholders (so that twelve would be a majority) might either 'ignore' the bill of indictment sent up to it, or return a 'true bill'. See Hayes, op. cit., pp. 357–63. An important exception to this principle at this period was the use of an *ex officio* information by the Attorney General to bypass the Grand Jury. An information was used in A.H. Rowan's case.

132. *Letters*, p. 204.
133. Punish for contempt. Irish Term Reports 285 at 286.
134. Ibid., p. 287.
135. Ibid., pp. 289–91.

declared, "I write this on my knee but my heart does not tremble, though my hand does."[136] It is no severe criticism of Drennan to suggest that the evidence of his post-trial conduct indicates that both may have been affected. The central break with the Society comes with his refusal to take or retake the Oath plus the new additions requiring secrecy. Looking back in 1797 at the estrangement that has taken place, he describes the singularity of his position to Martha McTier: "Is it not curious . . . that I, who of my own accord wrote the Test upon which the new associations are still, in chief, founded, should in pursuance of this same Test, be excluded and treated as a frigid neutralist, until I take it again in their form, and all this without the smallest change in my political principles or practice, except in not writing so as to throw myself, as other patriot suicides, into the gulf of a prison. . . ."[137]

Even before the end of June 1794 the effects of the trial were already evident. A reference had appeared in *Faulkner's Dublin Journal*, the Castle newspaper conducted by John Giffard, to the "demure doctor", accusing him of inciting rebellion.[138] This was plainly libellous and Drennan had received advice to that effect, but he had "had enough of law, and if ever I set foot in the Courts again it will be extraordinary." He did not however abandon politics; a stream of pamphlets and political verse indicate the range of his interests from the Union[139] to university education for Catholics and Presbyterians.[140] This is to say nothing of his professional life

136. *Letters*, p. 207.
137. Ibid., p. 250.
138. Ibid., p. 210.
139. See *A Letter to the Right Honorable William Pitt* (Dublin, 1799); *A Second Letter to the Right Honorable William Pitt* (Dublin, 1799); *A Protest from one of the People of Ireland against the Union* (Dublin, 1800).
140. See *A Letter to His Excellency Earl Fitzwilliam* (Dublin, 1795).

or his interest in journalism (as proprietor and writer)[141] and literature.

In the immediate professional downturn that followed his acquittal, his relatively straitened circumstances must have heightened his sense of isolation and vulnerability. This cannot have been helped by news of the conspicuous good fortune of John Pollock, who inherited a fine estate in County Meath from one of his clients.[142] Nonetheless Drennan had the sense to realise his good fortune in emerging intact from the monstrous if clumsy engine of eighteenth-century criminal law, a fact emphasised by the news that one of his cell mates in Newgate had been sentenced to death in July 1794.[143]

Despite the alteration in his political practice Drennan retained a loyalty to his erstwhile comrades. When he received a letter in April 1798 from Arthur O'Connor, then under trial for high treason in England, asking him to give character evidence at his trial, Drennan went to Maidstone despite the obvious cost to his practice from an extended absence.[144] On his arrival he discovered that John Pollock was already there giving background information to the Crown lawyers which could result in a highly damaging cross examination if Drennan were called as a witness.[145] Accordingly it was decided to dispense with Drennan's testimony and he returned from England with nothing more than the recollection of some conversations with the liberal *beau monde* and his usual sense of his own virtue.[146]

It is, of course, futile to speculate about the consequences of conviction, and the possibility of Drennan becoming in-

141. Of and in the *Belfast Monthly Magazine*.
142. PRONI Drennan Letters D591/613.
143. PRONI Drennan Letters D591/518.
144. *Letters*, pp. 272-3.
145. National Archives SPO Rebellion Papers 620/37/104; *Letters*, p. 274–5.
146. *Letters*, p. 276.

volved in the military plans of the later 1790s. When the loss to Ireland in terms of men of talent and integrity arising out of the execution of those plans is considered, it can only be a cause of some rejoicing that, as a result of his trial and acquittal, Drennan was preserved to make the contribution that he did in politics, medicine and education in Dublin and Belfast until his death in 1820.

Note on the Text

Unlike Rowan's trial which is found in a number of pamphlet editions[147] there is only one known edition of Drennan's trial, that published by John Giffard in July 1794[148] and printed by Rea and Johnson. The text has been altered only by slight imposition of typographical uniformity and modernisation of spelling and punctuation.

The text of the Intended Defence has been taken from that printed in Drennan's *Fugitive Pieces in Verse and Prose* (Belfast, 1815), subject to the same editorial criteria together with the omission of the footnoted encomium on the Revd Thomas Drennan which is not found in the first periodical appearance of the Intended Defence in the eighth volume of the *Belfast Magazine* (1811).

147. Professor O'Higgins gives four editions in *A Bibliography of Irish Trials and other Legal Proceedings* (Abingdon, 1986), p. 167.
148. PRONI Drennan Letters D591/517.

A
FULL REPORT
OF THE
TRIAL AT BAR,
IN THE
COURT OF KING'S BENCH,
OF
WILLIAM DRENNAN, MD

UPON AN INDICTMENT, CHARGING HIM WITH HAVING
WRITTEN AND PUBLISHED

A

SEDITIOUS LIBEL

WITH THE

SPEECHES OF COUNSEL, AND THE
OPINIONS OF THE COURT AT LARGE

DUBLIN:
PRINTED AND PUBLISHED BY
J. REA, 57, EXCHEQUER-STREET, AND
G. JOHNSON, 15, SUFFOLK-STREET.
1794.

TRIAL, &C.

In Easter Term, 1794, the Grand Jury of the City of Dublin, consisting of the following gentlemen,

Ald. Richard Moncrieffe,	William Humfrey, Esq.
— N. Warren,	Jas. Vance, Esq.
— W. Worthington,	John Norton, Esq.
— S. Reed,	H. Hutton, Esq.
— T. Tweedy,	A. Callage, Esq.
— J. Sutton,	Thomas Kinsley, Esq.
Sir T. Leighton, Bart.	H. Clements, Esq.
John Lees, Esq.	W. Stamer, Esq.
Jas. Ormsby, Esq.	James Magee, Esq.
Richard Manders, Esq.	Jonas Pasley, Esq.
Robert Powell, Esq.	Hugh Skeys, Esq.

found a bill of indictment against William Drennan, Doctor of Physic, as the author, printer, and publisher of a seditious libel.—The indictment contained nine several counts, charging him with printing and publishing in several different modes, the libel in question;—but as evidence was offered in support of only two of the counts, the second and eighth, it is unnecessary to recite the rest.

Indictment.

SECOND COUNT. — The jurors for our Lord the King upon their oath present and say, — That William Drennan, of the city of Dublin, Doctor of Physic, being a person of a wicked and turbulent disposition, and maliciously designing and intending to excite and diffuse amongst the subjects of this realm of Ireland discontents, jealousies, and suspicions of our sovereign lord the king, and his government, and disaffection and disloyalty to the person and government of our said lord the king, and to raise very dangerous seditions and tumults within this kingdom of Ireland, and to draw the government of this kingdom into great scandal and disgrace, and to incite the subjects of our said lord the king to attempt with force and violence, and with arms, to make alterations in the government, state, and constitution of this kingdom, and incite his Majesty's subjects to tumult and anarchy, and to overturn the established constitution of this kingdom, and to overawe and intimidate the legislature of this kingdom by an armed force, on the 17th day of December, in the 33rd year of the reign of our said present sovereign lord George the Third, &c. with force and arms at Dublin, aforesaid to wit. in the parish and ward of St Michael the Arch-angel, and in the county of the said city, wickedly, maliciously, and seditiously, did print and publish, and cause and procure to be printed and published, in a certain other newspaper called the Hibernian Journal or Chronicle of Liberty, a certain other false, wicked, malicious, scandalous and seditious libel, of and concerning the government, state, and constitution of this kingdom, according to the tenor and effect following, that is to say.

"The society of United Irishmen, at Dublin, to the Volunteers of Ireland, William Drennan, chairman, Arch. Ham. Rowan, sec. Citizen soldiers, you first took up arms to protect your country from foreign enemies, and from domestic disturbance; for the same purposes it now becomes necessary that you should resume them; a proclamation has been issued in England for embodying the militia, and a proclamation has been issued by the Lord Lieutenant and council in Ireland, for repressing all seditious associations; in consequence of both these proclamations it is reasonable to apprehend danger from abroad, and danger at home; for whence but from apprehended danger are these menacing preparations for war, drawn through the streets of this capital?" (meaning the City of Dublin), "or whence, if not to create that internal commotion which was not found; to shake the credit, which was not affected, to blast that volunteer honour, which was hitherto inviolate, are these terrible suggestions, and rumours, and whispers that meet us at every corner, and agitate, at least our old men, our women, and children?

"Whatever be the motive, or from whatever quarter it arises, alarm has arisen; and you, Volunteers of Ireland, are therefore summoned to arms, at the instance of government, as well as by the responsibility attached to your character, and the permanent obligations of your institution; we will not at this day condescend to quote authorities for the right of having and of using arms, but we will cry aloud in the midst of the storm raised by the witchcraft of a proclamation, that to your formation was owing the peace and protection of this island; to your relaxation has been owing its relapse into impotence and insignificance; to your renovation must be owing its future freedom, and its present tranquillity; you are therefore summoned to arms, in order to preserve your country in that guarded quiet which may secure it from external hostility, and maintain that internal regiment throughout the land, which superseding a notorious police, or a suspected militia, may preserve the blessings of peace, by a vigilant preparation for war. Citizen soldiers, to arms; take up the shield of freedom, and pledge of peace; peace, the motive and end of your virtuous institution; war, an occasional duty ought never to be made an occupation; every man should become a soldier in defence of his rights; no man ought to continue a soldier for offending the rights of others; the sacrifice of life in the service of our country is a duty much too honourable to be entrusted to mercenaries; and at this time, when your country has by public authority been declared in danger, we conjure you by your interest, your duty, and your glory, to stand to your arms, and in spite of a police, in spite of a fencible militia, in virtue of two proclamations, to maintain good order in your vicinage, and tranquillity in Ireland. It is only by the military array of men in whom they confide, whom they have been accustomed to revere as the guardians of domestic peace, the protectors of their liberties and lives, that the present agitation of the people can be stilled, that tumult and licentiousness can be repressed, obedience secured to existing laws, and calm confidence diffused through the public mind, in a speedy resurrection of a free constitution," (meaning that the people of Ireland had not at the time of publishing aforesaid a free constitution) "of liberty and equality; words which we use for an opportunity of repelling calumny, and of saying, that by liberty, we never understood unlimited freedom; not by equality, the levelling of property, or the destruction of subordination. This is a calumny invented by that faction, or that gang, which misrepresents the king to the people, and the people to the king, traduces one half of the nation to cajole the other, and by keeping up distrust and division, wishes to continue the proud arbitrators of the fate of Ireland.

"Liberty is the exercise of all our rights, natural and political, secured to us and our posterity by a real representation of the people; and equality is the extension of the constituent to the fullest dimensions of the constitution, of the elective franchise to the whole body of the people, to the end that government, which is collective power, may be guided by collective will, and legislation may originate from public reason, keep pace with public improvement, and terminate in public happiness. If our constitution be imperfect, nothing but a reform in representation will rectify its abuses; if it be perfect, nothing but the same reform will perpetuate its blessings. We now address you as citizens; for to be citizens you became soldiers; nor can we help wishing, that all soldiers, partaking the passions and interest of the people, would remember that they were once citizens, that seduction made them soldiers, but nature made them men. We address you without any authority, save that of reason; and if we obtain the coincidence of public opinion, it is neither by force nor stratagem, for we have no power to terrify, no artifice to cajole, no fund to seduce; here we fit without mace and beadle, neither a mystery nor a craft, nor a corporation; in four words lies all our power, universal emancipation and representative legislature. Yet we are confident that on the pivot of this principle—a convention, still less a society, less still a single man, will be able first to move, and then to raise the world. We therefore wish for catholic emancipation without any modification; but still we consider this necessary enfranchisement as merely the portal to the temple of national freedom. Wide as the entrance is, wide enough to admit three millions, it is too narrow when compared to the capacity and comprehension of our beloved principle, which takes in every individual of the Irish nation, casts an equal eye over the whole island, embraces all that think, and feels for all that suffer; the catholic cause is subordinate to our case, and included in it, for, as United Irishmen, we adhere to no sect but to society, to no creed but to christianity, to no party but the whole people. In the sincerity of our souls do we desire catholic emancipation; but were it obtained to-morrow, to-morrow would we go on as we do to-day, in the pursuit of that reform which would still be wanting to ratify their liberties as well as our own. For both those purposes it appears necessary that provincial conventions should assemble, preparatory to the convention of the protestant people; the delegates of the catholic body are not justified in communicating with individuals, or even bodies of inferior authority, and therefore, an assembly of a similar nature and organization is necessary to establish an intercourse of sentiment, and an uniformity of conduct; an united cause, and an united nation. If a convention on the one part does not soon follow, and is not soon connected with that on the other, the common cause will split into the partial interest, the people will relax into inattention and inertness, the union of affection and exertion will dissolve, and too probably some local insurrection, instigated by the malignity of our common enemy, may commit the character and risk the tranquillity of the island; which can be obviated only by the influence of an assembly arising from, and assimilated with, the people, and whose spirit may be as it were knit with the soul of the nation. Unless the sense of the protestant people be, on their part, as fairly collected and as judiciously directed, unless individual exertion consolidates into collective strength, unless the particles unite into a mass, we may perhaps serve some person or some party for a little, but the public not at all, The nation is neither insolent, nor rebellious, nor seditious; while it knows its rights, it is unwilling to manifest its power; it would rather supplicate administration to anticipate revolution by a well timed reform and to save their country in mercy to themselves.

"The 15th of February approaches; a day ever memorable in the annals of this country, as the birth-day of new Ireland. Let parochial meetings be held as soon as possible, let each parish return delegates, let the sense of Ulster be again declared from Dungannon, on a day auspicious to union, peace and freedom, and the spirit of the North will again become the spirit of the nation. The civil assembly ought to claim the attendance of the military associations, and we have addressed you, citizen soldiers, on this subject, from the belief that your body, uniting conviction with zeal, and zeal with activity, may have much influence over your countrymen, your relations, and friends. We offer only a general outline to the public, and meaning to address Ireland, we presume not at present to fill up the plan, or pre-occupy the mode of its execution; we have thought it our duty to speak, answer us by actions. You have taken time for consideration; fourteen long years are elapsed since the rise of your associations, and in 1782 did you imagine that in 1792 this nation would still remain unrepresented? 'How many nations in this interval have gotten the start of Ireland? How many of your countrymen have sunk into the grave?' In contempt of our said lord the king, in open violation of the laws of this kingdom, to the evil and pernicious example of all others in the like case offending, and against the peace of our said Lord the King, his Crown, and Dignity."

The other was a count for printing and publishing generally, omitting the words "Hibernian Journal," &c.

To this indictment Dr Drennan was in the same term called upon to plead.

The Hon. Mr Butler and Mr Emmett applied to the court for four days time to plead, and a copy of the indictment.

The Attorney General, on behalf of the crown, opposed the motion for time to plead, which he insisted was never allowed in case of an indictment.—As to the copy of the indictment, if Dr Drennan had, as his counsel contended, a right to it, he would obtain it of course without any such application as this now made.

The court was of opinion with the Attorney General and, Dr Drennan having been arraigned, traversed the indictment.

The 25th of June (in Trinity term) was appointed for the trial.

Wednesday, June, 25, 1794.

The court sate at half past ten; Mr Justice Boyd, having been taken ill, did not preside.

Dr Drennan appeared in court with his bail.

COUNSEL FOR THE CROWN,
  Right Hon. Prime Serjeant,
  Right Hon. Attorney General,

Solicitor General,
Mr Frankland and
Mr Ruxton.

Solicitor, Mr Kemmis.

COUNSEL FOR THE TRAVERSER,
Mr Curran,
Mr Fletcher,
Mr Emmett.

Solicitor, Mr Dowling.

The High Sheriffs returned the *Venire facias*, with a panel thereto annexed.

The panel having been called over, and twenty-six gentlemen having answered their names, the clerk of the crown proceeded to swear the jury.

Sir John Trail, Knt. was called.

MR CURRAN. My Lord, I understand that this gentleman has declared an opinion on the subject of this prosecution.

RIGHT HON. ATTORNEY GENERAL. I wonder to see these things practised again. I thought they would be ashamed of such artifices. I am sure the learned gentleman has been instructed to do this. These things are intended to go abroad, and have an effect on the public mind. If this is a cause of challenge — if it is law, that this is cause of challenge, let it be made — let us have the opinion of the court upon it.

MR CURRAN. My Lord, I stand upon nothing but the rule of law. If what I said be fact, surely he is not a proper juror to try the cause. If he has a pre-conceived opinion on the subject, I would put the question in the mode which the law warrants, by swearing the juror. It is true, he is not bound to answer any thing to his prejudice—but it cannot be to his prejudice to say that he has formed an opinion. Forming an opinion is not a culpable matter in our law; I, therefore, desire to have him sworn.

44

THE ATTORNEY GENERAL. The Gentleman has a right to challenge if he has good ground.

MR CURRAN. I move, my Lord , that Sir John Trail may be sworn to answer.

LORD CLONMELL. It cannot be done; it is not a legal practice.

MR JUSTICE DOWNES. I looked into the books on this point on a former occasion. It is laid down expressly in Hawkins, that this ought not to be done.

MR CURRAN. I cannot support the objection by any other evidence than the gentleman's own.

ATTORNEY GENERAL. Surely you might by your informer's testimony.

1. Sir John Trail was sworn,
2. Robert Alexander, Merchant, sworn,
3. Mark White, Merchant, sworn,
4. William Lindsay, Merchant, sworn,
5. Benjamin Woodward, Merchant, sworn,
6. Mark Bloxham, Merchant, sworn,
7. Peter Roe, Merchant, sworn,
8. William Beeby, Merchant, sworn,
9. Jeffrey Foot, Merchant, sworn,
10. James Hamilton, Merchant, sworn,
11. William Little, Merchant, sworn,
12. William Galway, Merchant, sworn,

The indictment was then read by the clerk of the crown, and Doctor Drennan given in charge to the jury.

The several counts were deliberately read, and the different copies of the libel scrupulously and accurately compared with the record by the traverser's counsel.

No variance however appeared.

Mr Ruxton opened the indictment.

THE RIGHT HON. THE ATTORNEY GENERAL. Gentlemen of the jury, in this case I am to prosecute on the part of the crown. The traverser stands indicted for making, printing, and publishing a seditious libel. I shall make no apology for being under the necessity of going over ground which I have gone over before, perhaps, tediously to the court. It is my duty to do so; it is yours, and that of the court, to hear it. And when I say it is your duty, I have little apprehension that you or the court will shrink from the task.

Gentlemen of the jury, Dr William Drennan stands indicted, for that he, being a person of a wicked and turbulent disposition, &c. [*here the Attorney General read the beginning of the indictment*] did on a certain day make, print and publish a certain false, scandalous, and seditious libel, of and concerning the government, state, and constitution of this kingdom,—with the views and intentions laid in the indictment.

There are nine different counts, or different modes of laying this charge in the indictment, in every one of those the libel with which the traverser is charged, is recited.

In laying this case before you, I shall observe particularly upon the several points which you are to consider. It will be your duty to enquire whether Dr Drennan was the publisher of the paper or not? Whether he was the author of it? For so he is charged. Whether he published it, with the views and motives laid in the indictment? And, finally, if you shall agree, that he is the author, printer, writer or publisher? Whether it is a libel against the laws, and against the peace of this country?

It will be my province to state the facts to you which evidence will support—I will make some observations upon the paper itself, which we assert to be a libel of the most dangerous and seditious tendency ever sent forth into the world, and upon which, if any one act had been done, the authors and publishers might now stand charged with the highest crime a subject can commit.

If upon the intrinsic meaning of this paper there can remain any doubt as to its tendency, the best interpreter it can have will be found in the history of the times in which it appeared.

And when I speak of this paper as a libel, I speak with that confidence which the unanimous opinion of this court, and the sober decision of a most respectable jury must give. This, however, should not affect you—though I am so clear in my opinion that it is a libel as to think it almost unnecessary to add any thing that cannot affect Doctor Drennan, for he is not yet tried.—I shall, therefore, lay before you and the court circumstances which will convince you that this prosecution is brought forward upon the best grounds, and for the good of the people in general.

I shall first consider the nature of that body of men from whom this paper proceeded, then the circumstances of the times in which it was promulgated, and next the evidence, by which, I trust, I shall bring home the fact to the traverser.

Gentlemen of the Jury, there had existed in the City of Dublin for some three or four years, a variety of clubs, under a variety of denominations, endeavouring to excite discontents in the people, and clamour and tumult against the laws and government of the country. They existed under several names, they changed their appearance with the times, as the people turned against them they altered their shape; but the agitators in the old clubs were always the leaders in the new.

At length they all combined under a new name, and supposing the circumstances of the times to be favourable to their hopes, in the year 1791 they formed the Society of United Irishmen, of all ranks, of all denominations, and all professions; most of them ignorant, I trust, of the principles and designs of their founders; for many were seduced to sanction their proceeding, some of them innocent farmers and graziers from the remotest parts of the country.

I say this that I may not be misunderstood to apply myself to those who have been unhappily for themselves misled

47

to become members of this society, without a knowledge of its scope and intention.

Even the few who at first constituted this body were not at the outset all acquainted with its objects. What those objects were, gentlemen, I will tell you;—to separate these kingdoms, and rouse the country into a flame.

Tending to these points, they published a variety of papers from time to time. The French revolution took place in 1789, after the formation of their constitution; those who had formed it, attacked it; from that moment their principles, their actions, were applauded, and even their frippery language was adopted, by the members of the club. When I state this to you, gentlemen, I do not mean to depart from my brief. This paper came from the society in its legislative capacity. The success of the French, in the campaign of the next year, had inspired those who before acted darkly, to appear openly. This city and this country, at one time, at the end of that year, stood exposed to massacres, such as have disgraced the name of France.

At that time subscriptions were set on foot to arm persons under the name of NATIONAL GUARDS, in a particular uniform, with pikes, and wearing buttons emblematic, if I may use the expression—of no royalty—the harp divested of the crown.

Such was the situation of your city, that no man who regarded property, who regarded good order, or who regarded religion, and saw these transactions, did not stand appalled with horror.—So passed the month of November, 1792. The promoters of sedition triumphantly appointed a day for mustering their troops. It almost appeared as if Government was terrified into silence by their audacity. The good and virtuous part of the people was alarmed at this apparent inattention, thus mistaking what was prudence for timidity. The ninth of December, 1792, was appointed for this muster of the National Guards.

Government, desirous of good men's approbation, waited to the last moment; avoiding to the last moment the necessity of exposing to danger the life of any individual, however criminal in his intentions he might be.

On the eighth of December a proclamation was published; a proclamation which, as long as our language or our history shall be remembered, will be regarded with reverence and respect.

To that proclamation we owe that at this day we possess the trial by jury; to that proclamation the traverser at the bar owes the protection which he receives this day from the laws and the justice of his country.

I am sorry to add that to it he also owes that he this day stands indicted at the bar.

The next day after this proclamation, the National Guards were to have met—perhaps to have taken possession of your City; but they were appalled—they met not—and the Society of United Irishmen was deprived of its prey. This Society naturally took extreme offence at this proclamation, for it put an end to that power which they flattered themselves they possessed, and which they were determined to maintain; this was on the 8th; the Society was in the usage of holding its conventions upon the Friday in each week,—the next Friday was the 14th—the Society assembled, to use a military expression, *in force*; sixty; seventy, or eighty members were present; it was thought necessary to encounter the force of government—of the kingdom,—the question was, whether the king and the antient constitution should stand, or these men, assembled in Back-lane, should be Lords of all?

This proclamation was a grievance to be redressed, and by any means—there belonged to the society a variety of committees—to take care of the property—the peace—the industry—the constitution of their fellow-citizens—committees of correspondence—of emergency, of laws—of constitution—every necessary appendage to a legislative body. To one of

49

these was this business referred; an address to the people was agreed on, to counteract the proclamation, or, to use their own cant "a counter proclamation was to be issued." The committee meet—they go aside to prepare this address— perhaps written long before: We charge that it was written by the traverser. The committee returned—Dr Drennan was in the chair, president of the convention for the day; Archibald Hamilton Rowan was Secretary. Dr Drennan, sitting in the chair of this convention, read aloud the libel which you have heard read and spelled over here this day. The question was put on every paragraph, the whole was agreed to, and ordered (Dr Drennan being in the chair) to be addressed to the Volunteers of Ireland. This will be proved to you beyond all question, and this being proved, it will be impossible for you to avoid drawing this conclusion, that it was with the traverser's authority this libel was published. I will add that every man then present was equally a libeller with him for the address passed unanimously, to counteract that proclamation to which we all owe so much. This address so agreed to, was still to be promulgated; a resolution was accordingly passed (the traverser still in the chair) that it should be published in three different papers— the Hibernian Journal, Dublin Evening Post, and National Evening Star, on three different days.

Mr William Paulet Carey, a printer, had been admitted a member of this Society, for it is a lamentable truth that the freedom of the press, the best guardian of your liberty and constitution, is perverted to the worst purposes, and that men adopt the publication of sedition and treason as a means of getting bread. Mr Carey was printer and publisher of the National Evening Star, and had probably become a member with a view to custom, and to be printer to the *Honourable* the Members of the Society of United Irishmen. He was desired to publish this paper; he requested the copy of it from the traverser; he was ordered to take it from the

Hibernian Journal, in which it could first appear. He was told by the traverser that the original must go to that paper, and that he might take his copy either from the Hibernian Journal, or McAllister's advertisement; for, Gentlemen, great pains are taken to disperse their publications; and, besides the newspapers, there were hand-bills dispersed to the number of many thousands over the whole kingdom, by every shopkeeper in this society, packed in his bales, by every merchant enveloped in his correspondence. If, then as I have stated, the traverser gave these directions, it establishes a connection between him and both the Hibernian Journal and the hand-bill.

Carey printed the libel three several times, and, to pursue critically and exactly his instructions, he procured the Hibernian Journal and the hand-bill. The Hibernian Journal was cut into pieces for the press, and delivered to the compositors, according to what is, I understand, the usual custom of printers.

If these facts are proved, they will show that the libel originated with Doctor Drennan—that he read it to the society—that he also, as a member of the society, adopted its sentiments, even were he not the author; and his direct orders to Cary to publish it will leave no doubt that he was the publisher himself in the Hibernian Journal; for when he directed Carey to take it from the Hibernian Journal, he adopted the Hibernian Journal as his own publication; and by this order to Carey became the publisher in the Evening Star.

As to McAllister's hand-bill, it has happened unluckily that, although one of them was affixed to the examinations, it has been lost in the crown-office.

Thus far, however, we shall be able to prove the publication by the traverser. We shall also prove that the printing of the libel in the Evening Star was paid for by the society, which, in the presence of the traverser, had directed the publication; that Carey made application to Mr Oliver Bond their secretary, who wrote an order to Mr Thomas Warren, their treasurer; (for the society has all those necessary officers). Carey applies to Warren, who says he is not now treasurer, but refers him to Mr Dillon, a woollen-draper in Francis-street; one or other of these gentlemen paid him, as for work done by order of the society, made while Dr Drennan was in the chair.

Thus much for the time, the occasion, and the person who published this paper.

It must appear, even to the most unwilling minds, that if this be proved, the traverser was the publisher of the libel in the Hibernian Journal, the Evening Star, and McAllister's hand-bill; and evidence will be also offered, tending to prove that he was the original composer of it, though that circumstance cannot much aggravate the crime, for every body present when it was unanimously agreed to was equally guilty; and the paper was so much the more dangerous as coming from so large a body. Every man assenting to the libel now read, is, by law, equally liable to prosecution, if it should be thought necessary to stretch forth the arm of that law over his head.

I feel a pleasure that it is not the printer I am now prosecuting for what, perhaps, his misery induced him to do, but that it is the original libeller; one who could not be actuated by such a motive, who must have acted from himself alone; and I rejoice that the punishment will, if he be convicted, go as near as possible to the primary cause.

I will now proceed to descant upon the libel itself though I feel that to be less necessary, as it is impossible that you must not have all heard and considered it in the repeated discussions it has received, both in and out of this court; but these prejudices you cannot bring here; you will take it with you into your jury-room when you retire, and there consider whether it was written for fair, cool, and deliberate discussion of public measures, which every man has a right so to discuss, or with intent to over-awe the government, to counteract the proclamation I have mentioned, or to force the legislature into any particular measure, good or bad; and this you will consider upon the internal evidence of the paper itself.

It sets out with the pretence of advising a reform in parliament, and professes to address the antient Volunteers; every libel has some pretext or cover and, on a former occasion, to this object the attention of the jury was very ingeniously drawn.

No man here disputes the right of every subject to discuss all constitutional questions—it is an undoubted right which he who presumes to violate should be cast with disgrace out of the country. This right it is the duty of juries to protect and preserve inviolate, whenever the hand of power is lifted against the freedom of the press. This freedom is violated in this case—not by this trial, but by the seditious practices of this society; and if the traverser appears to be guilty, and you find him so, you will preserve that freedom which he has attempted to violate.

This paper goes directly to disgrace government, by charging it with the most abominable acts—it goes to force the legislature to enact new laws—it goes farther—it calls together a National Convention—critically pursuing the French plan—and this paper is the mandate—the writ of summons for the purpose; and when I say this is the object, let me be adjudged by the libel itself. Carry into your jury box the most ingenious of its justifiers, and if any of you be convinced that it will bear any other construction, let the traverser be acquitted. It cannot be; upon this subject the philosopher and the old woman will have the same sentiments. Discussion or reform are not the objects of this libel; but the promoting an assembly to control that legislative body by which we are governed. This libel, not content with advising delegates and parochial meetings, does what kings dare not,—what no officer, however oppressive or tyrannical, has ever dared in this country—what no man has ever been bold and wicked enough to do, such force and energy have our free laws; what the wickedest person in the state dare not, this body, without power—this unlawful body and which, while my tongue can vibrate, I will call so—has called an assembly, purporting to be the representatives of the people, and dared to order the armed Volunteers of Ireland, pretending (what they did not feel) that they addressed the antient Volunteers, to assemble round this Convention at Dungannon. Why a Convention? To petition parliament! What could they want with the armed Volunteers of Ireland; Is it necessary to ask?—Let us for a moment see what would have been the effect of this object.

We, quiet and peaceable inhabitants of the country, exerting our talents and our industry for ourselves and our families, advancing the weal and commerce of the country, conceiving that we lived under a constitution fixed and settled, a constitution till of late, since the divisions in France, envied by all the world; we, conceiving ourselves protected by a king and magistrates, see on a sudden the representatives of the mass of the people of Ireland, rich and poor, great and small, without the consent of the supreme power, assembled at Dungannon to model, as may best please them, the old constitution. We are appalled—but when we see armed bodies attending them, what shall we do? either take arms ourselves, or sink at once, while every thing dear to us was destroyed—and we saw the constitutional powers controlled by this new authority.

I say again, gentlemen, and I wish to impress it on your mind, that every man has a right, and I hope we will long exercise it, of discussing political questions—but not in such language as it calculated to excite tumult and sedition; and I hold it impossible, that when you take this paper into your chamber, you can put any other construction on it than that which I contend for.

From the society of United Irishmen, of which Dr Drennan, as chairman, was the head, many such inflammatory papers have issued, and in consequence of them your city has stood exposed to such dangers as no city, save Paris, ever saw. Government, by their proclamation, preserved it, and with a view to that proclamation was this libel published, imputing to that proclamation the destruction of public credit, which had been falling fast before the efforts of this society, and was upheld by the proclamation. To it also this paper imputes the tumults which pervaded the country, and throughout every occasion is taken to stigmatize the established powers. It was known to be the intention of the government to establish the Militia; which has, thank God, been since established; and men, whose only design was, forsooth, to reason, became terrified at the idea of a Militia, though they saw danger at home and abroad. A Militia was not, indeed, hostile to their avowed intention—reform; but it was to their real one—the destruction of the established constitution; and a Militia is accordingly reviled. The Police, another institution for public protection, is also libelled. At one time an attempt is made to seduce the army, and at another it is disgraced to excite the people against them; so that they will be found to have libelled every power by whom they thought government would be enabled to oppose them. All this will be found in the libel; and it is needless in me to dwell on a subject which can be so perfectly understood.

I will conclude with observing, that the intent and purpose of this paper was to prevent the operation of the proclamation; but of this you are to judge; and though I assert that every paragraph in that paper is libellous, yet it is your province to consider and pronounce an opinion on it.

Gentlemen, there are nine different counts, as they are called, in the indictment.

The *first*, for printing and publishing in the National Evening Star of the 20th of December, 1792, the libel in question.

The *second*, for printing and publishing in the Hibernian
Journal of the 17th, for by directing Carey to copy that
paper, he avowed the publication.

The *third*, for printing and publishing on the 20th.

The *fourth*, for printing and publishing on the 17th.

The *fifth*, for printing and publishing on the 20th.

The *sixth*, for writing and publishing on the 20th.

The *seventh*, for publishing on the 20th.

The *eighth*, for publishing on the 17th.

The *ninth*, for publishing on the 20th, with some variance.
I shall now produce evidence to support the charge. When
the traverser has adduced evidence in his defence, his Majesty's
Prime Serjeant will observe upon the whole of the case.

First witness. Mr William Paulet Carey, sworn.

Examined by the Prime Serjeant.

Q. What is your name, Sir?

A. William Paulet Carey.

Q. Do you recollect, Sir, the month of December, 1792?

A. I do.

Q. Did you in that month attend any, and what meeting,
of any Society?

A. I did, a meeting of the Society called the Society of
United Irishmen of Dublin, held in Back-lane.

Q. Were you a member of that Society, or only a visitor?

A. I was a member. I believe no visitors are permitted to
attend the meetings of the Society.

Q. Do you know any of the persons who were present at
that meeting?

A. I believe, Mr. Archibald Hamilton Rowan was present.
Of this I am not positive.

MR CURRAN. Sir, you have no right to give evidence
against a man who is not here.

COURT. It is not evidence.

Q. Was Dr William Drennan there, Sir?

MR CURRAN. I object to that question. It is evidently a
leading one.

56

Q. By the Court. Do you know Doctor Drennan?

A. I do. There he is, my lord; he was at that meeting.

Q. Did he take any particular part in the transactions of the meeting?

A. I heard him read a paper from the chair to the Society.

MR CURRAN. My lords, is the charge to be borne forward by this kind of interrogation; here have been four questions put, and three of them illegal.

Mr Carey, in continuation.

My recollection of the progress of the night is extremely faint. There has been a considerable lapse of time, but I have had reason to recollect since—until then I had no particular reason to remember it—I had reason to recollect the particular publication, but not the proceedings of the night.

Q. What particular publication do you mean, Sir?

A. I mean the paper commonly called the Address of the Society to the Volunteers of Ireland.

COURT. Mr Prime Serjeant, keep him to the particular paper.

Q. Was there a question put on that paper?

MR CURRAN. My lords, my lords, surely this is a leading question—it may be answered by yes or no!

MR JUSTICE CHAMBERLAIN. Certainly any question which suggests the answer is a leading one.

PRIME SERJEANT. My lord, with great deference—

MR JUSTICE DOWNES. Every question is improper to which the answer may be *yes* or *no* merely.

PRIME SERJEANT. My lords, I bow to the court, though I take the true distinction to be where the question infers a fact, the answer to which will criminate the party accused.

Q. What was done then, Mr Carey?

A. A question was put on the paper, which Doctor William Drennan had read; it was after some debate.

COURT. By whom was the question put?

A. By Doctor William Drennan.

57

COURT. What do you mean by the *question?*

A. This question was addressed to the Society: "Shall this stand as the address of the Society of United Irishmen of Dublin, to the Volunteers." It was passed in the affirmative.

COURT. What do you mean by that?

A. I mean that the Society acceded that it should stand as their address, in the customary manner of *ayes* and *noes*. There were no *noes* that I recollect.

MR CURRAN. Mind, gentlemen,—they acceded by ayes and noes, and there were no noes!!

MR CAREY. I spoke as to the form, not as to the fact.

Q. What was the next step?

A. A question was then put to the Society by Doctor William Drennan, that the address should be printed, and published in the Dublin Evening Post, the National Evening Star, and the Hibernian Journal.

COURT. How was that disposed of?

A. In the same manner as the former. In the affirmative.

Q. What happened then?

A. There was a conversation between me and Doctor Drennan that night. I was about to quit the Society.

COURT. About to leave it entirely?

A. No, my lord,—to leave the room; and Doctor William Drennan desired me to take the address of the Society to the Volunteers from the Hibernian Journal, or Tom McDonnell's paper; I can't say which or——

COURT. For what purpose was this order?

A. To insert it in the National Evening Star,—it was from the Hibernian Journal of the ensuing Monday, to insert it three times. I was printer and proprietor of the Star. The order was alternative—"or from McAllister's hand-bill, to insert it in my paper.

COURT. How do you mean, to insert it three times?

A. In three successive publications.

Q. What time was this?

A. It was the fourteenth of December, 1792.

COURT. What do you mean by McAllister's hand-bill?

A. It was a copy of the same publication, printed on half a sheet of paper. I saw it the next day, or rather late the next night. It was in that I read it first.

Q. Are you sure it was the same paper read by Doctor Drennan?

A. When I read it, I recollected the title and matter; I knew the connection and relation between it and the paper I had heard read. I read it also in the Hibernian Journal; they were all the same words and matter, published in different forms.

Q. Did you say the words were the same?

A. I did, the same as the news-papers and hand-bills, as I *then* recollected and thought.

MR CURRAN. Sir, you must swear directly and positively, or not at all.

MR CAREY. I saw the hand-bill and the Hibernian Journal; it struck me that it was the same paper from the relation and connection I saw between them.

MR CURRAN. My Lords, is this fair evidence to go to a jury?

COURT. Have done, Sir, with relation and connection. You have sworn that they struck you to be the same—were they so?

MR CAREY. My Lord, I cannot swear they were copied word for word.

PRIME SERJEANT. Proceed, Mr Carey.

A. The next day I sent the Hibernian Journal up to my printing-office in consequence of the directions I had received, with orders to my men to copy the address.

Q. What time was this?

A. This was on Tuesday the 18th; the Hibernian Journal was printed on the Monday.

COURT. For what purpose did you send it up to your office?

59

A. To have it inserted in my paper.

Q. Was it so inserted?

A. It was published in it on Tuesday evening—the same day. I directed a second publication on the 20th.

PRIME SERJEANT. This, my Lord, is the day of publication laid in the indictment.

Q. Have you any copy of that publication?

A. I have. [*Shows a newspaper.*] This is the National Evening Star.

Q. Who published that paper?

A. I did. I swear this was published by me. It was printed by my journeymen and artists.

Q. What is the date and title of it?

A. The date is December the 20th; the title, the Rights of Irishmen, or National Evening Star. It contains the address of the Society of United Irishmen of Dublin, to the Volunteers of Ireland, inserted by the directions of Doctor William Drennan, and in consequence of his order.

Q. Were you ever paid for the advertisement, and by whom?

A. I sent my apprentice, John Whitaker, to Mr Oliver Bond, some time after, with a bill for the insertion of different publications of the United Irishmen; the three first were the address to the Volunteers. My apprentice did not live with me, but he gave me the amount the next time I saw him.

Q. What kind of paper was that read by the traverser,— was it printed or manuscript?

A. It was manuscript.

COURT. In whose hand was it?

A. In Doctor Drennan's, my lord. I mean he held it in his hand. I don't know whether it was his hand-writing.

Q. What was the title of it?

A. It was "an address," or "the address," I have not the exact words, "of the society"——

MR CURRAN. Sir, you must not give evidence of belief, you must swear positively,

A. It was the address of the Society of United Irishmen to the Volunteers.

Q. What was done with that paper?

A. Doctor Drennan said the copy he had was wanting for another paper. I cannot be positive; but I understood it was for the Hibernian Journal.

Q. What became of that Hibernian Journal from which you copied?

A. I cannot exactly tell; such papers are generally cut up into scraps, and distributed to the different compositors.

COURT. What did you say the traverser said about the manuscript?

A. That it was wanted for another paper.

Cross examined by Mr Curran.

MR CURRAN. Sir, I have few questions to ask you; you will answer, I am sure, most conscientiously. Were you a member of this society?

A. I was.

Q. Had you been long so?

A. I had for a considerable time before.

Q. Pray, Sir, did you ever offer to print their proceedings without payment?

A. I did—I beg leave to explain the reason.

MR CURRAN. Oh, Sir! you have explained sufficiently.

SOLICITOR GENERAL. Surely there never was an instance of a witness being refused leave to explain his answer.

MR CAREY. The society of United Irishmen, at a time I received notice of a prosecution—I believe your lordship's name was signed to it.

MR CURRAN. What, Sir, a prosecution against your *own* person? I never heard of it before.

MR CAREY. I think your lordship's name was to it. I am sure it was. No! it was not; it was signed by the Attorney General. I received notice of a prosecution intended against me, for an article copies from the Northern Star. The society

61

resolved to support me. I was grateful, and offered to publish for them *gratis*. I wrote this to the society, who thanked me; but answered, that it was better the expense should fall on the whole society than on an individual.

COURT. What did you say the society resolved?

A. To support me under this prosecution. I, in gratitude, made this return. In gratitude, I offered to print for them.

MR CURRAN. Why, Sir, you surprise me much by saying, that *you* were considered criminal by Government. Was it a mistake?

A. I received a notice, and attended at his Majesty's——

MR CURRAN. At his Majesty's !!!

A. Hear me out, Sir—at his Majesty's Attorney General's house, to show cause why a prosecution should not be instituted against me.

Q. And the Lord Chief Justice's name was signed to the notice?

A. I told you I was not positive.

COURT. Was it so or not?

A. My recollection is, that your lordship's name was to it—I believe it was.

Q. When was this?

A. Early in November; before the 14th of December, 1792.

Q. What then, it was not for this publication?

A. No; it was a former prosecution on account of publishing the Belfast Rejoicings. This was an order on me to show cause.

Q. What sort of a paper was this notice,—what did it contain?

A. I do not recollect the substance of it—it was a small piece of paper.

MR CURRAN. So, Sir, of a paper containing a friendly hint to you of an intended prosecution, which might have deprived the public of your *sacred* person, you cannot recollect a word, and yet you swear to this paper as the same which Doctor Drennan read.

A. Sir, I have sworn that I received the notice, and that I think his lordship's name was to it.

Q. Do you say then that it was to it?

A. I do not swear to the fact?

MR CURRAN. Will you give me an answer, Sir—was it or was it not?

A. I cannot say.

MR EMMET. Did you not say that you could not swear it was not to it?

COURT. One at a time, gentlemen.

MR CURRAN. Will you give me an answer, Sir?

A. I did receive such a notice.

Q. Cannot you form a belief whether the name of the Chief Justice was or was not to the paper?

A. I cannot.

Q. Tell me, Sir, whether it was or was not? Give me a direct answer either way.

A. I believe—I think it was.

MR CURRAN. There is nothing, I see, like giving you an election, you have made choice of an answer at last. Did you not say a while ago you could not with certainty form a belief?

A. I cannot tell whether I did; I don't remember what my answer was; repeat the question, if you please.

MR CURRAN. Answer first, Sir.

A. I cannot, till you repeat your question—I do not remember it.

Q. What, Sir, you that can recollect what passed in 1792 so well, can't remember what happened within these five minutes?

A. I cannot.

Q. Was there any prosecution intended against you for the present publication?

A. There was one depending.

Q. Did you publish it?

A. I have sworn that I did.

Q. And pray, Sir, how came *you* to do such a thing as publish a libel?

A. I relied upon the *Lawyers* in that society that they would not bring forward any measure which they thought liable to bring people into a prosecution.

Q. Then, Sir, is it your opinion that the intentions of the society in making this address were honest?

A. I did not say that.

Q. Were your own intentions honest?

A. I believe I have no right to answer that question.

Q. Why do you think so?

A. My counsel here say I have not.

SOLICITOR GENERAL. The court will certainly protect the witness.

MR CURRAN. The question is a fair one—answer me, Sir. Do you think the intentions of the Society were honest?

A. It is merely matter of opinion what I think the intentions of the Society.

PRIME SERJEANT. Sure he has no right to answer the question. You have no right to enquire into the motives of the Society, since you objected to speaking of persons who were absent. Doctor Drennan is the only subject of consideration now.

COURT. We think you have a right to answer the question?

MR CAREY. I believe the intentions of the Society were *originally* to look for a reform in parliament; which I look upon as an honest intention.

MR CURRAN. Sir, you have not answered me yet, as to what you believe were their intentions in this instance?

A. It is merely matter of opinion; but since you must have the truth, I believe they were to raise an armed force in the country to act against the constituted authorities. This is my opinion now.

Q. Sir, I don't ask your opinion now, but what it was on that night?

A. I believe those were their objects on that night. I did not say it was my opinion on that night.

COURT. Repeat the answer to the last question?

A. I believe their intention was to raise an armed force to act against the constituted authorities, and obtain a reform by force. I swear this as a matter of belief.

Q. Was this your opinion at that time?

A. I don't recollect that I thought so then. I don't think I did.

Q. Pray, did you not yourself make a motion in the Society to take up arms?

A. I did. My reason was that I thought the Society should show itself as prompt to arm and share danger, as to excite others. It was not a motion, it was only notice of one. I thought the Society should not thrust men forward into danger, and shrink from sharing it themselves. It did not come to motion—I merely mentioned my intention to make such a motion.

Q. Did any one oppose this project of yours?

A. The person who spoke against converting the Society into an armed body was the man who moved this address from the chair—it was Doctor Drennan. It was proposed when the Volunteers were trod down.

Q. Really, Sir, I do not recollect any such event—about what time did it take place?

A. It was some time after the proclamation. I deemed it but fair, that those who had instigated should support them, and share the danger; but Doctor Drennan answered that it was the cause of the Volunteers only; and that the Volunteers should protect their own honour.

Q. Was this the night on which the address was agreed to?

A. It was not; it was some time after the Volunteers were put down.

Q. What danger was this you proposed to share?

A. That those who had called them to arms, should share with them the danger.

Q. And pray, Sir, did you think was this motion of your a proper one?

A. I did not think it *proper*, but I thought it honest.

Q. Really, Sir, this is a new distinction—between honest and proper.

A. I mean that I thought it not *prudent* though honest.

Q. Go on, Sir?

A. I conceived it honest, that if any ill consequences fell out, they should come forward with whom they originated. I meant it as a touchstone to discover character. I wished to ascertain character—and I did so; for those who were readiest to call on others were most backward themselves; they wished to play a safe game, and to hold off.

Q. So then, Sir, your scheme for arming was rejected by the Society?

A. Their objection was not by any means to a general arming, but to the particular danger which might rally round their own persons. It was a safer game for themselves to withhold from arms.

Q. Who do you mean by *themselves*, Sir?

A. I mean Doctor William Drennan and the lawyers of the Society; those in particular took the lead; they wished to hold back and keep out of the business, whatever the consequences might be.

Q. Then, Sir, your motion was disapproved?

A. Doctor Drennan declared that as to the Volunteers it was their own cause, and they should take care of their own honour.

Q. And, pray, what was your motive?

A. I wished to try their sincerity. I saw men thrusting others forward into a situation, which I knew they would not share themselves.

Q. Were you sincere in this proposal?

A. I was. He threw the Volunteers on themselves to protect their honour. As an individual, he did not wish to incur hazard—as such I *did*.

COURT. What do you mean by "as an individual?"

A. I mean *personally*, my lord; but that he did not disapprove of others doing so.

Q. How long did you continue a member of the Society after this?

A. Until November, 1793.

Q. How long was that?

A. Nearly a year after.

Q. What then? This was in November, 1792?

A. It was not. I cannot remember the date exactly.

Q. Why did you continue so long a member of a Society, whose conduct you condemned?

A. I stayed in the hope that it would keep its word with me in supporting me under prosecution. I conceive it broke its word with me in that instance.

Q. What time did you begin to condemn the Society?

A. From the time I saw them depart from their principles; for when I had published a libel on government, Mr Simon Butler——

[*Here the witness was desired to mention no names.*]

——A gentleman,—a lawyer told me that as the libel expressed that Ireland had no constitution, which he said was the truth, I should be supported; for he said——

MR CURRAN. Sir, I desire you will not repeat the conversation or the names of any person not now in question. Conversations are not evidence.

COURT. Surely, in many cases they are, to explain the principal question; for instance, in murder, they are admitted to prove who was last with the person?

MR CURRAN. My lord, I am only counsel for the traverser, not for the Society of United Irishmen.

MR CAREY. I condemned them——

Q. When did you begin to condemn them—tell me the time?

A. I was——

Q. Good God, Sir, cannot you give me a direct answer, you that can remember so accurately?

67

A. I cannot tell the precise time. If you will let me explain.

ATTORNEY GENERAL. Sure you may allow him, Mr Curran, to ascertain it by circumstances.

COURT. Indeed, Mr Curran, you have made a great deal of his recollecting at a great length of time—so much that it will go to the jury—you may let him state circumstances.

MR CAREY. The reason I condemned the Society was this; when I received the notice I attended the Committee of Constitution at a lawyer's house. I was asked what part of the libel had been fixed upon. I pointed out a part on which the Attorney General had made a mark with his pen. The lawyer approved the principle, and said we had *no* constitution, and that I ought to be supported; for that if such bold truths were not to be told, the Society must fall. I was told that I should be supported; but an outlawry has been almost sued out against me. I condemned the Society also when I saw it turned into a borough, to list into notice two or three *unpractising* professional men.

COURT. What do you mean by this expression *unpractising?*

A. Two or three persons of profession, who wished for practice and had it not. This was done by seducing a few thoughtless persons. It was only my particular situation which prevented me employing whatever talents I may have, in exposing them.

Q. If the society had supported you, would you have come forward as an informer?

A. I cannot answer that question, *it would be drawing on futurity.*

Q. Sir, I want no prophecy; I only wish to know whether if they had supported you, you would have appeared here this day?

A. That is mere matter of opinion, I cannot form an opinion.

Q. Did you ever call upon the society to support you?

A. I called on them to fulfil their promise, but it was cheaper to pay their engagements by my expulsion than support.

Q. Now answer me, Sir, directly, do you prosecute here this day from malice to the traverser, as the mover of your expulsion?

A. I declare, in the presence of God, that I have not the smallest malice to Doctor William Drennan, and that I do not prosecute out of a motive of malice. I conceive myself to come forward like a man who has received a forged note, and gives up the primary cause.

Q. Pray, friend, do you think that you will be prosecuted yourself?

A. I conceive I will not?

Q. Have you had a promise to that effect?

A. No, not a direct promise; but I understand I will not.

Q. Were you ever arrested in consequence of this publication?

A. I was, I lay a whole night in a police-house.

Q. How do you know it was the same publication?

A. I was told it was, and I believe it was; I proposed that the society should pay my bail, that I might leave the country.

Q. And what was the consequence?

A. Every effort I made for the purpose was fruitless. I could have run from my bail; one of them gave me leave to do so; the other knew the society better, and would not assent to it.

Q. And yet, Sir, you say you had no malice against the traverser?

A. I said no such thing. I said that I did not prosecute from malice, not that I never had any malice against him; for I heard——

MR CURRAN. Sir, your hearsay is no evidence.

COURT. Surely he may explain why he ever had malice against the traverser.

69

Q. Sir, I ask you again, have you any malice against the traverser?

A. Let me explain why.

MR CURRAN. My lord, I contend for it that he has a right indeed to explain an answer when it is given, but no right to introduce his belief upon collateral matter before he gives an answer.

COURT. He has not a right to ramble into impertinence, but he has a right to tell the grounds of any malice he may have. Had you any malice to the traverser?

A. I deemed the action a base one. I did not wish to injure him; I wrote him word that it was base in him to move my expulsion, when I was just about to be tried for the publication. I was angry that he had done so; but I did not wish to injure him.

MR CURRAN. Sir, you have not answered me yet; have you, or have you not, malice to the traverser?

ATTORNEY GENERAL. He has given an answer.

Mr Curran. Fellow, will you answer me or not?

A. If you will explain the word *malice*, I will. I was angry with him, but I would not take an unfair advantage of him.

Q. Did you ever say you would be revenged of him?

A. I never did. I often said that, as the origin of the publication, he should meet the danger first.

Q. Did you not say you would be revenged of him?

A. I never made use of the expression.

Q. You say Dr Drennan desired you to publish an address—did you read it that night?

A. I did not.

Q. Had you it in your hand?

A. I had not.

Q. Did it contain these words,—"William Drennan, chairman, Arch. Ham. Rowan, sec."?

A. I stated the fact at first—that—

Q. Sir, I say, answer me—were they or not in it?

ATTORNEY GENERAL. Really, my lord, the man is answering as nearly as possible every question; the court will, I hope, protect him.

MR CURRAN. What! here a man comes as an *informer*; in such cases the court should indulge every latitude of examination. If the counsel for the crown interrupt me with another word, I will sit down. Answer me that question.

A. You put a question to me, and while I was answering, you interrupted me. I state that the address published in my paper I saw and knew to be the same paper which was read in the Society, This I say, on my oath and recollection.

Q. Will you swear that those words were in it?

A. I heard him read the paper,—I believe—

Q. Sir, I don't want your belief. Were those words of address in it?

A. Let me see the paper.

Q. I will not. Were these words of address in it or not?

A. I heard a paper read, and I am asked, whether a certain set of words were in it? I cannot swear they were.

Q. Did you hear him read these words? [*Reads the first sentence.*]

A. The words I heard were towards the close of the paper, and the question was put on its standing the address of the society of United Irishmen.

Q. Were these words in it:—"to protect your *threatened* country from foreign enemies?"

A. I told you already.

Q. Answer me, Fellow!

A. I cannot remember these particular words or phrases.

Q. On your oath, did the traverser read those words?

A. I suppose he did.

Q. By the virtue of your oath, did you think I asked you as to your belief?

A. I cannot swear it.

Q. Can you swear to these words? [*Reads another sentence.*]

A. I cannot swear positively to his having read any particular sentence.

Q. Was there any part of that which you published, read?

A. I recollected some particular sentences. I recollected them at the time—it has lain by me ever since.

A. Will you swear positively, that you published any one sentence word for word as he read it?

[*Witness hesitates.*]

Question repeated.

A. I have stated the fact as it was, I cannot give any other answer.

Q. What, Sir, then you cannot swear it?

A. Give me leave to answer—I published it immediately after.

Q. Are you not, on your conscience, avoiding my question?

A. I am not.

Q. Answer then!

A. I published it after having read it.

Q. Sir, answer me; have you not laboured to avoid my question?

A. I am not positive. I did not take a note book to note it down; and therefore I demur to that question.

Q. You demur; do you?

A. I demur to answering it.

Q. What then, Sir, you can and you cannot; you can swear, and you cannot swear to the paper; what am I to understand?

COURT. He was assigning his reasons.

A. The traverser desired me to publish the address to the Volunteers from the United Irishmen, from the Hibernian Journal.

Q. Was it the same paper he read that was published by you?

A. He desired me to publish it from a certain paper, which I did; I also got it in McAllister's hand-bill.

Q. Where is that hand-bill?

A. It is lost.

Q. Where did you get the [*Dublin*] Hibernian Journal?

A. I sent one of my lads to McDonnell's office for it—I can't say which of them.

Q. Did that paper contain the address which the traverser read, word for word?

A. I cannot answer directly to that question—it was published from the Hibernian Journal, which I sent up to my printing-office.

Q. Were you with the compositors—can you swear that they even copied the [*Dublin*] Hibernian Journal exactly?

A. I was not—I did not compare them.

Q. Did you read it in the [*Dublin*] Hibernian Journal yourself?

A. I did not—I read the title of the address, and sent it upstairs.

Q. Can you swear that it was a genuine [*Dublin*] Hibernian Journal?

A. I cannot be positive.

Q. Can you swear to any one paragraph as read by Doctor Drennan?

A. I cannot.

Q. You cannot swear to the address either?

A. I can only on belief—I cannot swear to the exact wording.

Q. By virtue of your oath, are you as anxious to give evidence in favour of the traverser as against him?

A. I am not willing to change the facts; what I recollect, I assert. Am I bound, my lord, to answer this question?

Q. Sir, answer me the question directly?

A. I don't understand it.

LORD CLONMELL. Let me put it. Are you as willing to give evidence that shall acquit, as to convict the traverser?

A. I am.

Mr Curran. Sir, you are a well dressed, and I should suppose, a tolerably educated man; tell me, did you mean to answer my question?

A. I did not understand it as first; as soon as I did I answered.

Q. Why then, Sir, if you did not understand it, why did you ask the court whether you were bound to answer it?

A. I was at a loss on the subject; it appeared to me to be the same question you asked before, whether I had malice to Doctor Drennan.

Q. Can you swear to any one paragraph as read by the traverser?

A. I cannot.

Q. Nor to any in the Hibernian Journal?

A. I cannot.

Q. Will you swear to the paper used by your compositors?

A. I cannot. They are in court, and will answer you themselves.

Q. Have you talked, friend, of this business to any one?

A. I have to every one I met.

Q. Now, friend, friend!! by virtue of your oath, I desire you to answer me this question, and it shall be the last: Would you have appeared here this day to prosecute, if the society had kept its word with you?

A. Upon my *word*——

Q. Upon your *oath*, Sir,—keep your word for more solemn occasions abroad; answer me?

A. I would not have given up Drennan if the society had kepts its engagement with me.

Q. Yet, did you not say a while ago, you could not form an opinion; that you could not look into futurity? go down—

A. I have been so baited with questions, that I have been put beyond myself; I never was in a court before but once, and then only a listener.

FOREMAN OF THE JURY. Sir, the jury desire to ask you a question: Had you ever any conversation with Doctor Drennan on the subject of that paper, after the night he desired you to publish it? Did he at any time make objections to the accuracy of the publication?

MR CURRAN. Good God, my lords, this is an illegal question. Gentlemen of the jury, it is not law.

FOREMAN. It is a question deduced from his direct answers; I would not for the world put an improper one.

MR CURRAN. There is an idea of deference to a jury gone abroad beyond what the law allows; I cannot suffer such a question to be asked?

ATTORNEY GENERAL. My lord, I submit that this is a fair question. Dr Drennan was present when resolutions were passed adopting the address, and directing it to be published in the papers; surely it is reasonable to ask this question, flowing from the evidence already given.

MR CURRAN. He has not proved who employed him, nor even who paid him; he has talked about Mr Bond on hearsay.

FOREMAN. I understood his answer to be that he sent his boy with a bill for this publication or libel, or whatever it is, the subject of this trial, and that the boy brought him back the money.

Mr Thomas McDonnell called and sworn.
Examined by the Solicitor General.

Q. Are you the printer and publisher of a newspaper in circulation in this city?

A. I am a printer and bookseller.

Q. Of what paper are you the printer?

A. [*To the Court.*] My lord, I submit, whether I ought to answer this question? There is at this moment a prosecution depending against me as printer of the Hibernian Journal.

COURT. It is the universal practice, when a person is asked a question, the answer to which may cast a reflection on himself, that he may refuse answering.

75

Q. Are you, Sir, the printer of any newspaper?

A. Have I a right to answer, my lord?

MR CURRAN. My lord, the man is not bound to answer?

ATTORNEY GENERAL. The counsel for the prisoner has no right to interfere between us and our witness; if he will say that he will tell the truth, I will enter a *nolle prosequi* upon the prosecution against him here in court this moment.

MR CURRAN. What will not the court interfere to prevent the timidity of a man from ruining him?

MR JUSTICE DOWNES. Sure the Attorney General's offer cures that.

MR CURRAN. But it will not save him from private actions?

COURT. After what he has said "that he is under prosecution as printer of the Hibernian Journal," it cannot be allowed to ask him whether he is so or not.

ATTORNEY GENERAL. Mr Kemmis, draw up a *Nolle prosequi* in this case of McDonnell; and if he has no objection to answer, I can't think the traverser's counsel have a right to interfere?

MR MCDONNELL. My lords, I have no objection to answer your lordships.

The Nolle prosequi *was then drawn up,*
signed, and filed in court.

MR CURRAN. In point of law, my lord—

ATTORNEY GENERAL. Is Mr Curran your counsel, Mr McDonnell?

MR CURRAN. I will be your counsel, if you please, Mr McDonnell.

COURT. The court will hear you, Mr Curran, as to the competence of this witness

MR CURRAN. Sure the man may be allowed to have counsel.

SOLICITOR GENERAL. This is the first time I ever heard of a witness's counsel. If every witness was to have counsel to sift every question that might be asked there would be a total stoppage of justice.

COURT. Have you anything to offer as to the incompetence of the witness, Mr Curran?

MR CURRAN. I only say, that the court will be circumspect where a man is called upon to answer questions by which he may entrap himself criminally.

ATTORNEY GENERAL. We all understand what the learned counsel has thrown out; it can have no effect upon us.

Examination resumed.

Q. Are you printer of a paper in this city?

A. I am printer of the Hibernian Journal.

Q. Where was *this* paper printed [*Shows a newspaper.*]?

A. At my house, I believe.

MR FLETCHER. Sir, your belief will not do.

Q. Are you acquainted with the type of Hibernian Journal?

A. I am.

Q. Does any other person print the Hibernian Journal?

A. I believe no other does; I am sole proprietor of it.

[*A large volume of newspapers was then produced.*]

Q. Do you know this book?

A. I do; it is mine. These are the papers of 1792; they are bound for my use; they are bound at the end of each year. They are sent to a book-binder, and bound.

SOLICITOR GENERAL. My lord, we are going to offer McDonnell's book in evidence, to make use of one of the papers in it. Did you get these papers safe from the binder again?

A. They were returned bound according to my directions.

Q. Is that one of your papers? [*Pointing out one.*]

A. I believe this is an Hibernian Journal of mine.

[*Answer objected to as upon belief only.*]

Q. Did you ever hear of any other such paper in Ireland?

A. I never heard, or knew, or saw one but mine.

Q. Have you any other sets of them bound together?

A. I have many other volumes of the Hibernian Journal.

Q. Are they made up in the same way

A. They are sent out to the book-binder at the end of each year to be bound.

Q. Were you applied to, to insert an address of the Society of United Irishmen to the Volunteers?

A. There have been such addresses published in my paper.

Q. Were you applied to, to insert such an address as this?

MR CURRAN. This indictment is laid in the tenor, and not to the purport or effect; they must prove the tenor; the answer to this question cannot be evidence, one way or the other.

COURT. You cannot support it, Mr Solicitor.

Q. Were you applied to, to publish an address, importing to be the address of the Society of United Irishmen to the Volunteers?

A. There was an address of that import left at my house in my absence, on a Sunday, the day previous to this paper's being published; it was taken by a person in my house; I was not at home.

Q. When you went home did you see it?

A. I found such a paper left at my house.

MR CURRAN. This is mere hearsay evidence;—he found a paper at his house!

Q. Was this paper published?

A. There was a publication in my paper of the address of the United Irishmen to the Volunteers.

Q. Were you ever paid for that publication by the United Irishmen?

MR CURRAN. What has that to say to the traverser?

SOLICITOR GENERAL. It has been proved that it was agreed to when several were present, that it was read by the traverser, as chairman, my object is to show that the traverser adopted it as his own.

MR CURRAN. Carey did not swear that any person but Doctor Drennan was present.

SOLICITOR GENERAL. Where was *this* paper printed?

MR CURRAN. Answer positively upon your oath, Sir.

COURT. We will not suffer him to answer improperly.

MR McDONNELL. It was printed by me, I believe.

MR FLETCHER. Sir, you must answer point blank, it was or was not.

SOLICITOR GENERAL. Are you sure this is the same you printed?

MR McDONNELL. I don't think anything was put into it since.

SOLICITOR GENERAL. My lord, we have a person here from the Stamp-office, to swear to a particular paper.

Francis Lestrange sworn.

Where did you get that paper?

A. From Mr McDonnell.

Q. What employment are you in?

A. I am register of pamphlets in the Stamp-office. This is McDonnell's paper. I got it for the Stamp-office, according to act of parliament.

Cross examined.

Q. Was it on the day of publication you got this?

A. I cannot say it was.

Q. Are you sure it is the same paper you got?

A. I am. I got it from McDonnell himself. I signed my name on it.

Q. Where has it been ever since?

A. Lodged in the Stamp-office.

Q. [*To McDonnell.*] Did you deliver this paper to Mr Lestrange at the Stamp-office?

A. I never go to the Stamp-office to deliver papers.

LESTRANGE. I got it from McDonnell himself in his shop.

SOLICITOR GENERAL. Did you ever deliver any paper as yours to Mr Lestrange, which was not so?

MR McDONNELL. I never delivered to him or any other as the Hibernian Journal, any paper which was not published by me.

Q. Were you paid for this address?

A. I believe I was.   [*Objected to.*]

Q. Who was it charged to?

A. The society of United Irishmen.

Q. Compare this paper with that on your file,—do they correspond?

MR CURRAN. This is a question for the jury to decide, if these papers can go up to them.

MR JUSTICE DOWNES. If it is a question for the jury, Mr Curran, it must be open to evidence.

SOLICITOR GENERAL. One witness swears that he got the paper from McDonnell; who swears that he never gave as the Hibernian Journal any paper which was not a real one. Have you ever seen the traverser?

A. Frequently in the street.

Q. Was it after the publication of the address?

MR CURRAN. He has proved no publication.

SOLICITOR GENERAL. Have you seen Dr Drennan since December, 1792?

A. I have in the street.

Q. Have you elsewhere?

A. I have. I saw him in the society of United Irishmen.

Q. Have you ever seen him in your own house?

A. I cannot say he was ever in my house but yesterday; he was yesterday in my parlour, looking over this volume of newspapers.

Q. Did you converse with him about this prosecution?

A. We did not.

Q. Did you hear Carey's evidence?

A. I did.

Q. Were you in the society on the night of which Carey spoke?

MR CURRAN. Oh! Mr Solicitor! in mercy to those against whom we have heard that the power of the law may be exerted, do not ask these questions.

MR McDONNELL. I was not present that evening. I never saw the paper until it was in print, or heard of it till it was left at my house.

SOLICITOR GENERAL. I have done with you, Sir. My lord, we contend, that under this proof, it is competent to give this paper in evidence.

Mr McDonnell cross examined by Mr Curran.

Q. Can you swear that a paper, calling itself the Hibernian Journal, or Chronicle of Liberty, could not be printed by any other man but yourself?

A. Any man possessed of the same types and paper might do it.

Q. Can you swear that you gave this identical paper to Lestrange?

A. I cannot: he is in the habit of coming to my shop, and taking away papers for the Stamp-office.

Q. Can you swear that this identical paper was published by you?

A. I cannot swear it; but I have every moral certainty of it.

MR CURRAN. Sir, I want none of your morals.—Then, Sir, your evidence is shortly this, that you cannot say positively that you published this paper.

John Whitaker examined by Mr Frankland.

Q. Do you know William Paulet Carey?

A. I do.

Q. Were you his apprentice, and employed to collect his accounts at any time?

A. I was his apprentice in February, 1793, and employed to collect his money for newspapers and advertisements.

Q. Do you recollect receiving money from any particular person for him?

A. I cannot recollect the names of all the persons.

Q. Did he ever send you to Mr Bond?

[Question objected to]

A. I received money from several.

SOLICITOR GENERAL. We submit, my lord, that we are entitled to read this paper.

MR JUSTICE CHAMBERLAINE. Out of whose hands does it come?

SOLICITOR GENERAL. Out of Lestrange's who got it from McDonnell. Dr Drennan desired the printer of the Evening Star to take a certain address from the Hibernian Journal, of which McDonnell has sworn himself sole proprietor.

MR CURRAN. The objection has not been made to it yet, and if it were we should be heard first.

SOLICITOR GENERAL. Certainly; I thought it had been made.

MR CURRAN. The question is so plain, that I think it ought not to be debated. I object to reading this paper.

This is an indictment at the suit of the crown, for a libel. A question is made, whether this newspaper can be read in evidence against Dr Drennan, the traverser, in order to be sent to the jury, who are to try the fact of guilt, or innocence; and it is narrowed to this ground—has there been such a body of evidence laid before you, as, if proved, establishes such a privity between my client and this paper, that the question of guilt, or innocence, should be decided by its contents? The nauseous theme of credibility is not now before you.

Carey said, and he is the material witness, that he was at a meeting of the United Irishmen, where he did not swear to the presence of any individual but Dr Drennan; that Dr Drennan read an address to the persons present; no one is named; that a question was put on a paper, as an address of the society; that it passed in the affirmative. As to the paper, he could not swear to a single phrase stated in the indictment; he never read the manuscript—he never had it in his possession—he could not swear that it was truly read, or, that a single paragraph of what he heard was in the paper.

82

I have recapitulated the evidence without the smallest error. On his cross examination he said the orders given to him were to copy the address *so read and agreed to*. I hear learned gentlemen *say no*—I am warranted in asserting the affirmative; for there is no alternative, unless you can suppose that he had a general order to print anything he pleased; but he printed it from McAllister's hand-bill, and the Hibernian Journal. No man can bind himself to be responsible for a future publication which does not pursue his orders literally; in this case it is impossible to fix criminality, because he has not sworn to the tenor of a single phrase. McAllister's paper is out of the question; we shall therefore say nothing upon that subject.

Supposing all that Carey said to be perfectly credible, which is a question yet remaining, we have no proof that he copied the Hibernian Journal for which he sent his boy; that paper does not appear. Indeed he has told you it was cut into scraps. What did he say,—"I never read that paper; I don't know whether the compositors acted on it accurately." Is there one word here to bring guilt home to the traverser?

But not to rest on Carey's evidence, the printer of the Hibernian Journal is called; he cannot swear that he printed that paper—any other man might have done it. Can the guilt or innocence of a man rest on such evidence—or go to a jury on the belief of a prosecutor. The evidence of Lestrange cannot affect Dr Drennan—the act of a third person with the printer. One would rather suppose that Lestrange, like some incautious trader, had drawn upon his memory without any effects in her hands; for McDonnell believes he did not give the paper to Lestrange. This is the evidence.

If Carey has said anything to prove a privity between the traverser and the paper, has he, in the wildness of his vagaries, said that this is even in substance the paper read by Dr Drennan.

Suppose the paper was read, and appeared to be such a libel as it has been called; did he compose it—did he publish it—speak to the printer—to the compositors—not one word of evidence is adduced. Is it on similarity of types—on the colour of ink—that you sentence a man to two years imprisonment? God help you all, if the likeness of types or paper is to be brought in evidence against you.

Gentlemen press this to go to the jury. I appeal to their learning—their ingenuity—their anxiety for public justice, is there any one point proved upon which, if true, a jury can convict my client? It comes to this, whether dark surmises, and obscure suspicions, shall supersede the old wholesome laws which require positive proof.

It cannot be; and I trust your lordship's decision this day will put a stop to the scandalous torrent of oppression, and those prosecutions which are to the scandal of society; I trust that you will not hestitate to say that such evidence shall not go to a jury.

EARL CLONMELL. As to the prosecutions to which you give such hard names, Mr Curran, they must have been before some other court; there have been none such before me.

MR CURRAN. My lord, I allude to prosecutions before your lordship's colleagues—

EARL CLONMELL. Mr Solicitor General, we call on you.

SOLICITOR GENERAL. My lord, as to those prosecutions in which I have been concerned——

MR CURRAN. I assure you, Mr Solicitor, I never alluded to any gentleman, particularly my friends.

THE SOLICITOR GENERAL. I trust that it is not necessary for me to vindicate the government of the country, or the officers of the crown, against the imputation that has been cast upon them in the prosecutions that have lately been instituted; the necessity of their institution, and the moderation with which they have been conducted, are not subjects of argument; and to such subjects only I wish to apply myself, and to call your lordship's attention. Two points have been made by the traverser's counsel; one, that the identity of the Hibernian Journal, now offered in evidence, has not been proved in such way that it should go to the jury; the other that no evidence has been offered to establish a privity between Dr Drennan and this paper which can warrant the court to suffer it to be read as against him. Let us see how these objections can be supported. McDonnell proves that he is sole proprietor of the Hibernian Journal; that there is no other paper of that appellation in this kingdom. Lestrange swears that he got this very paper from McDonnell in his own shop; McDonnell swears that he never gave any paper as the Hibernian Journal, which was not a genuine publication; and that Lestrange is in the habit of calling for papers at his shop. The next point is the privity between Dr Drennan and the paper in question. It has been established that the paper was printed on the 17th December, 1792. Carey has proved that Drennan directed him on the 14th, to copy from the Hibernian Journal that should be published of the 17th; and it is ascertained that a question was put by Drennan from the chair, whether the publication in question should be inserted in the Hibernian Journal of that date. Carey then proves that he did publish it in his own paper from an Hibernian Journal, which identical paper we might have had here, but that it was cut up for the press.

So that it appears that Doctor Drennan, by anticipation, had adopted the publication of this paper in the Hibernian Journal, while he kept the original manuscript in his pocket. I say, then, that you not only have evidence to go to a jury of the identity of the paper, and of the imputable privity with the traverser, but you have the very best evidence that can be supposed in a transaction of the kind. If this species of evidence is inadmissible, the prosecution of libellers would, in most cases, be hopeless indeed, however deeply such publications may affect the comfort of individuals, or the public tranquillity.

From the mysterious secrecy with which the authors of such mischief are usually concealed, it is not one case in a thousand that can furnish such satisfactory proof as the present; and here the only question is, whether there is evidence to go to the jury which can justify the reading of the newspaper which is offered. If it should be refused, it would be a determination that would shake the established law of evidence in matter of libel, at a time when not only the crown, but every good subject, is more materially interested than ever to have its energy preserved. And let me observe, my lords, when gentlemen talk of the prosecutions of the crown, that the law of evidence is the same, whether the crown or individuals are concerned.

Suppose a man intending to libel the Chief Justice of the kingdom should read an address to him in the presence of hundreds, and proclaim that the publication would be inserted on a certain day, in a certain paper—shall it be said that this would not be evidence, that the publication when made should not be imputable; because the original paper was not produced, or a direct conference with the printer was not proved.

Suppose it proved that a body of men had agreed to commit a certain crime, and the act should be done afterwards, at the time, and in the manner concerted, surely proof of their agreement and conversation would be evidence to go to a jury against any of those who so conversed and confederated, on an indictment for having procured the crime to be committed, as in the present instance.

We are told that it is not proved, that this accords with the original paper read by the traverser. I say it has been proved, that the traverser has the original that was resolved on. Show us the paper, and show us your innocence.

A jury-man, with that perspicuity and strength of mind which I have long known him to possess, asked, whether Dr Drennan had ever had any conversation with Carey, the witness, after the publication, to disclaim it, or otherwise? I say, if in the course of such conversation the traverser has not disclaimed the publication, it must go with irresistible impulse to the jury. Another circumstance, tending to show the traverser's privity, has been proved by McDonnell; that he was yesterday, the day before the trial, at his house, searching and reading over the file of newspapers that has been produced.

As to the identity of his Hibernian Journal, there can be no doubt. I contend for it that the traverser's direction for taking the copy from this paper establishes a privity between him and the publication in this paper, and is strong evidence to go to the jury for that purpose.

EARL OF CLONMELL. The question in this case is—

PRIME SERJEANT. My lords, I am ready if necessary.

EARL OF CLONMELL. We are with you, Mr Prime Serjeant.

MR FLETCHER. If the court is of opinion against us, I hope to be indulged with a word.

EARL CLONMELL. If we were not clear—if my brothers had any doubt, or did not concur, we should, perhaps—but we can hear only one on a side.

There are nine counts in this indictment—one for publishing a libel in the Hibernian Journal.

See what is the evidence. It is proved—I mean it is sworn to by Carey—that on a certain night the traverser was chairman of a certain Society calling themselves United Irishmen; that he read a paper upon which a question was put, that it should be adopted as the address of the Society to the Volunteers of Ireland—that this was carried unanimously— that he got directions from the traverser to publish this address— and adds he, "you will find it in the Hibernian Journal of Monday," "or Tom McDonnell's paper." Suppose he had not read the paper, but repeated it from memory, and had said, "you are to publish this." (This question of credit is withdrawn from this argument.) "Where shall I find it"—"In Tom McDonnell's paper on Monday." Would not this be evidence? Here he put it in his pocket—it was ordered to be published in the Hibernian Journal; in the Star and the

Evening Post. The next man produced swore himself sole proprietor of the Hibernian Journal. His name is McDonnell; he could not, however, ascertain the identity of this paper. Lestrange was then called. McDonnell proved that he had been in the habit of getting the paper at his shop; that he never delivered any—not the Hibernian Journal. Lestrange swears he delivered him that paper, he swears it positively, that he got it as the officer of the Stamp-office. For my part, I cannot see how it is possible to connect circumstances more closely together. The question is not now as to the weight of evidence, that is for the jury. It is sworn that this paper was got from McDonnell; he swears that he is sole proprietor of the paper; the question is, whether it can be read as his paper: if it is, it was the model to which Drennan referred Carey—the Hibernian Journal of next Monday. I think there is ample foundation for allowing it to go to the jury.

Justices Downes and Chamberlaine concurred.

The libel was then read from the Hibernian Journal, or Chronicle of Liberty, of December 17th, 1792, and attended to by the traverser's counsel with scrupulous accuracy.

Mr John Bell (fifth witness for the crown) was then called and sworn.

Examined by Mr Ruxton.

Q. Do you know Dr Drennan?

A. I have seen him.

Q. Do you see him in court?

A. I do; there he is.

Q. Do you recollect December, 1792?

A. I do.

Q. Were you at any meeting on the 14th of that month?

A. My lord, I this day heard the Attorney General say that every man present at that meeting was equally culpable with the traverser; I beg to know, therefore, whether I ought to answer the question?

COURT. The better way, Mr Attorney, is that the witness should be freed from his apprehensions.

ATTORNEY GENERAL. There is no prosecution against him and such assurance as I can give, he shall have; and it is that there is no thought or supposition of a prosecution against him. If he desires a pardon too, I shall recommend him; but all this does not remove the *possibility* of a prosecution.

COURT. Are you content with this, Mr Bell?

A. I am.

Q. What business do you follow, Mr Bell?

A. I am a cotton manufacturer.

Q. Do you recollect the 14th of December, 1792?

A. I remember that night I was at a meeting of the Society of United Irishmen, held in Taylors-hall, Back-lane.

Q. Did you see the traverser there?

A. I did. He read a manuscript paper from the chair; he put the question from the chair, that it should stand the address of the United Irishmen to the Volunteers of Ireland.

Q. How did he read it, all together, or by paragraphs?

A. He read it in the usual way. I cannot tell whether it was all together, or paragraph by paragraph?

Q. Was any other question put?

A. I cannot take on me to say that any other was put.

QUESTION BY THE COURT. How was the question put?

A. It was, whether it should stand as the address of the Society of United Irishmen; or of that Society to the Volunteers of Ireland?

Q. Was there any other question or address moved?

A. I cannot take on me to say positively that there was.

Cross examined by Mr Emmett.

Q. Where did you see this paper?

A. In Dr Drennan's hand.

Q. Did you read it?

A. I did not.

Q. Did he read what it contained, word for word, from the paper?

A. I cannot take upon me to say that he did.

Q. Did he read these words,—"Address to the Volunteers of Ireland"?

A. I believe he did not.

Q. Did he read these words,—"William Drennan, chairman, Arch. Ham. Rowan, sec."

A. I believe he did not; it would, I think, have been nonsense for him to read those words, if I may venture to submit my opinion.

Q. Will you say that that paper (taking in the title) was word for word, the address he read?

A. I cannot. If you ask as to my belief, I must give you my reasons.

Q. You cannot say then that those words were in the paper?

A. I cannot say that the names of Drennan and Rowan were in the paper—I believe they were not read.

ATTORNEY GENERAL. We have closed on the part of the crown.

Thomas Traynor, first witness for traverser, sworn.
Examined by Mr Fletcher.

Q. Do you know Mr William Paulet Carey?

A. I do.

Q. What are you, Sir?

A. I am a merchant, and live in Poolbeg Street.

Q. Had you ever any conversation with Carey respecting the traverser?

A. I had. I was mentioning to some person that I thought Carey was much aggrieved; and that I would set on foot a subscription for his relief——

Q. How long since is this?

A. This was about the first of April last; I did not know Carey before; he waited on me next day, he told me he was much obliged to me for my intention; that he had been much aggrieved by the United Society of Irishmen; but that if they would pay his bail, he would quit the kingdom: he added, that he did not like either to turn informer against Drennan or lose his liberty, and that a few guineas would be of infinite service to him.

Q. Did he threaten the traverser at all?

A. He said that if he did leave the kingdom, he would give Drennan a *flailing* before he went; said I, "Drennan is a delicate little man, and a stroke from a strong man would kill him;" he answered that, *by Jesus*, he would think it no crime to assassinate such a villain, who had ruined his peace for ever, and made a motion to expel him from the United Society of Irishmen, just at the time they should have supported him; some time after this I heard Dr Drennan was taken up.

Q. Did you see Carey at any time after?

A. He never came near me since.

ATTORNEY GENERAL. You may go down Mr Traynor, I shall not cross examine you.

Second witness for the traverser. William Wooloughan, sworn.
Examined by Mr Curran.

Q. Do you know William Paulet Carey?

A. I do.

Q. Do you recollect any conversation with him at any time?

A. I do. As to the way he was situated as to the Society.

Q. How long ago was it?

A. I cannot tell. I never expected to be brought to court about it.

Q. Was it three months ago?

A. I am sure it was, if not more.

Q. Do you recollect his saying anything about the traverser?

A. I do not recollect anything in particular of the traverser; but I hear he said——[*objected as hearsay.*]

Q. Do you know anything of your own knowledge?

A. All I know I will tell in a few words: Carey said several times, that if the Society of United Irishmen deserted him, he must desert them; but that he would not, if they would exonerate his bail, and let him quit the kingdom.

Q. Did he say anything of Dr Drennan?

A. I heard him say Dr Drennan used him very ill; he seemed to have a very contemptible opinion of the leaders of the Society.

ATTORNEY GENERAL. You may go away, Mr Wooloughan.

Third witness. Thomas Wright sworn.

[At the request of a juror; he kissed the book.]

He was examined by Mr Emmett.

Q. Do you know William Paulet Carey?

A. I do.

Q. Had you ever any conversation with him about a publication in the Star; and what was it?

A. I have had many conversations with him on different subjects; I had one about the address to the Volunteers.

MR EMMETT. Mr Wright, you will be cautious to answer no question so as to criminate yourself.

A. I met Mr Carey after that address had been agreed to; he told me that he had been neglected by the gentlemen of the committee of correspondence; he asked me if I was of that committee—I was not—in their not sending to him—in not providing him with the paper that he might publish it.

COURT. What address do you mean?

A. I believe it was the libel for which Mr Rowan was convicted.

Q. How long was this after the 14th of December?

A. It was but a few days; the Tuesday after I expressed my surprise that his paper had been overlooked, as I knew of his letter and offer to publish all their writings *gratis* in his Journal; and I thought such an offer deserved, at least, such attention as that the paper should be sent to him.

Q. What else did he say?

A. He said that he had no instructions for publishing the paper as early as any other person, and that they had not treated him well. He then consulted me whether he should publish it or not, and wished for my directions as to it. I said I thought he was bound by his former writing and request to the Society to give all their publications *gratis*. He then consulted me as to the copy he ought to pursue, having no original. I said the Hibernian Journal was, in my own opinion, most correct; but that I was not qualified to give him an opinion on the subject, not being one of the committee.

MR EMMETT. That certainly is not evidence either way. We have done with you, Mr Wright.

Cross examined by the Solicitor General.

Q. What time did this conversation take place?

A. Some days after the 14th of December.

Q. On what days was the Star published?

A. On Tuesdays, Thursdays, and Saturdays, I believe.

Q. What time was the original publication read?

A. I don't know; I know nothing but what I have said.

Q. I ask you as to your belief, was it not on the 14th?

A. I cannot recollect; I have no memorandum.

Q. Have you ever heard that it was read at the Society.

A. I have.

Q. Have you heard whether Dr Drennan was in the chair of that meeting?

A. I don't know whether I have a right to answer that question.

SOLICITOR GENERAL. Sir, I have a right to your hearsay and belief?

A. I have heard he was; I believe he was?

MR EMMETT. When you speak of the address, Mr Wright, it is of something word for word with another thing, not anything which you see here.

SOLICITOR GENERAL. Have you not heard, and do you not believe, that the traverser, at that meeting, read an address to the Volunteers, which afterwards appeared in the Hibernian Journal?

A. I have no belief either way, or other.

Q. Was this the title of it? [*Reads the title.*]

MR EMMETT. Word for word, Sir.

SOLICITOR GENERAL. Is this to be borne, my lord?

COURT. This is a very improper interruption; you have no right to say to a witness, you must say so and so, and nothing more.

SOLICITOR GENERAL. Is this the same paper?

A. I believe not; for there were some alterations made in it. According to the mode of the Society, there never is a paper produced by a committee, which does not undergo alterations.

Q. Was there any question put upon these alterations?

A. I believe there was, according to the usage of the Society.

Q. You recommended the Hibernian Journal as the most correct; was it that you thought it so?

A. It was evident on looking into the Evening Post, that it was not correct there; it was nonsense in many parts.

Q. How did you *know* that it was correct in the Hibernian Journal?

A. I only allude to correctness in the style; for I do not know that the matter was the same read in the Society. I told him it was more correct in composition in the Hibernian Journal than in the Evening Post.

Q. How do you know then that there were alterations in it?

A. I have known many things so altered that I thought it improper to publish them, in my apprehension.

Q. You talked of *committees*—what did you mean?

A. There are several committees belonging to the Society.

Q. Sir, you must have heard much of this remarkable publication; cannot you form a belief as to the author of it?

A. I never troubled myself to enquire or know.

Q. How many constituted the committee of correspondence?

A. Five.

Q. Were they elected by the Society at large?

A. I do not know.

Q. Do you say, Sir, that you cannot form a belief as to the author of this remarkable paper?

A. I was as indifferent as to that paper, as any other that ever came from the Society.

MR EMMETT. What did you mean by its being more correct in the Hibernian Journal?

A. I meant as to style, composition and good English.

Q. You are a surgeon, Sir?

A. That is my business.

Q. Pray, are not the proceedings of the Society published correctly in the newspapers of the day?

A. When I was employed to publish for them, I published as they desired me, most commonly in the Evening Post.

Q. Did you see this publication in any other paper or form?

A. I saw it in various newspapers, and in McAllister's hand-bill.

Q. Did you read these words—"Dr Drennan in the chair"?

A. I did.

Q. Did you ever meet him afterwards?

A. Often.

Q. Did you never ask him if he was the man mentioned as chairman?

A. Never.

Q. Had you any doubt on the subject?

A. I do not think my conjecture a thing on which to convict any man. I do not wish to involve any gentleman, Doctor Drennan or any other; my coming here was merely by chance.

Q. Did you read this paper?

A. I do not think I did.

Q. What! and you recommended it as correct?

A. What! when I saw it was nonsense in the Evening Post, should I not recommend to a man asking advice, what was correct in preference to nonsense?

Q. Did you read these words—"Doctor Drennan in the chair?"

A. I do not recollect that I did.

Q. Did you understand that to mean the traverser?

A. I could understand nothing else.

[*Evidence closed.*]

MR CURRAN. Of the nine counts, which do you rely on, gentlemen?

ATTORNEY GENERAL. On that charging the publication in the Hibernian Journal, and on the general one, the 2nd and 8th.

The record was then read in part by the clerk.

MR CURRAN, *after attending some time, said,* I believe there is no such variance as I understood there was.

My Lord and Gentlemen of the Jury, I am of counsel for Dr Drennan, the traverser; and, gentlemen, I do not, for the sake of my client, regret that my state of health prevents me trespassing long on your time, or that of the court; for my heart tells me that if he is reduced to stand in need of any effort from talent, that it is impossible, under the circumstances of the case, that he can hope for any assistance from an advocate, where, if there is any danger of conviction, it must arise from what passes in the minds of the jury, and not from anything which has passed in this court.

It may be a loss to the traverser that he is not aided by the personal exertions of those who are connected with him by habits of life and uniformity of pursuits. Such a person I am not; to him I am a perfect stranger. I never, to my knowledge, exchanged a word with him save once in the public street. I never was under the same roof with him that I know of; and the reason why I yielded to an ordinary application to become his counsel was because I had been personally defamed for acting as counsel in the defence of another who was charged with the same libel. I felt that my character in the world, little as it may be, was owing all to my professional talents; and I feel that, if a barrister can act so mean and despicable a part as to decline, from personal apprehension, the defence of any man accused, he does not deserve to be heard in any court of justice.

I will state shortly what I conceive the question to be, and the evidence brought in support of the charge.

The indictment is that Dr Drennan, the traverser, did publish the libel, and that he did print and publish the paper, with the base and seditious intentions there stated. To this he has pleaded not guilty; and one question to be tried is, did he, in point of fact, publish the paper? The next, upon which I shall trouble you but very little, is as to the nature of the paper, whether it is a seditious libel or not?

The law of libels in this country, and in Great Britian, has lately, by the perseverance and exertions of two men [Mr Fox and Mr Erskine] at last crowned with success, undergone a most fortunate change.

There is said, gentlemen, to be an instinct in animals, which directs them to those medicines which relieve their disorders; and it seems as if, in the public malady of the three kingdoms, this only medicine had been discovered, and carried into effect by this law.

For part of the court which I address, I have infinite regard and esteem—to extend that profession would perhaps be as presumptuous, as it would flatter my vanity, but let me not by this be understood to profess any contrary feeling; I merely disavow the arrogance of affecting to feel, where I have no claim to any interest.

But gentlemen, the law has taken the power of decision in those cases from the court, and vested it in you. And you are not only to enquire into the fact of publication, but into the question of "libel or not." Upon the latter question I have said I would make a few observations; but I will be frank with you, and will say, that if you have any disposition to believe the fact of publication, I would advise the traverser to prepare with a fatal facility to receive your opinion, that the paper is whatever the prosecutors please to call it. For, if you believe it, it must be from some perversion of mind—some gangrene of principle, with which I disdain to hold parlance or communication; and this I say, from a proud conviction, that there will be no law in this country when such monstrous facts are swallowed by juries, and the country disgraced by such convictions.

As to the liberty of the press, I have heard, and I have read of some things relative to it lately, at which I am truly astonished. I have heard that an English Attorney General should say, "that the guilt or innocence of a man depends on the candour with which he writes." I feel that this must have been an imposition; I cannot believe that it could have been said. The liberty of the press does not consist in reasoning right—in candour—or weighing the preponderancy of arguments, as a grocer weighs his wares; it is founded in the principle that government is established for the happiness of the people; that the people have a kind of superintendant or inquisitorial power, to watch over government, that they may be satisfied that the object is truly sought. The liberty of the press is not for expressing merely argument, but to convey the feeling of personal discontent against the government, that the passions of the governors may be checked; and if any one is bold enough to tell them they overbound their duty, they may be tortured into rectitude, by being held up as objects of odium, abomination, horror, or ridicule.

If you confine the liberty of the press to fair argument; if you condemn as libellous, every publication where invective may be a little too warm, where it may go beyond the enormity, or, the complaint beyond the grievance—you destroy it.

Every man knows what is a public crime; the maliciously pointing out grievances so as to disturb the quiet of the country; such a crime will never find protection from a court or a jury. If the traverser did intend "to diffuse among the subjects of this realm, discontents, jealousies, and suspicions of our sovereign Lord the King, and his government; disaffections and disloyalties to his person, and government, and to raise very dangerous seditions and tumults within this kingdom," &c. he ought to be found guilty—if he did not, he is entitled to acquittal. Having said this, I dismiss the subject; because, I trust in God, so fatal an example to the liberties of this country, as a condemnation upon such evidence, will never be given.

What has Carey sworn,—that he was at a meeting on the 14th of December, that Dr Drennan was there, that the question was put on an address, that he himself was desired to publish that address, that the manuscript could not be given him, but that he should take it from the *Dublin Journal* of the next Monday—that he sent for that paper; a great deal of his evidence went to proving the Star, but that was not read, and is out of the question. The question is therefore narrowed to the publication in the *Dublin* Journal; is there any evidence that this was the paper read in the Society? No! What is it?—Carey has told you—indeed he told you the impossibility of his swearing it; I read the address in the paper—he could not swear even to the substance, he could not tell that it was the same. Coiling and twining about me, as you saw that wretched man, he could not prove this; therefore, all the evidence on the part, comes to this, that Dr Drennan did produce some address in that meeting, but of what it contained you have no evidence before you. And, as to the publication in the Hibernian, the evidence is so vague, that it can give no aid whatever to the former proof. So that the evidence stops at the meeting in Back-lane.

I asked Carey what address he was desired to publish—he answered, that agreed to by the Society; what proof have

* It is evident that Mr Curran meant the Hibernian Journal—but these were certainly his words.

you that he did so—it will be ingeniously endeavoured to impress upon your minds that a general power to publish was given by the traverser to Carey, and that he thereby made himself personally liable for Carey's acts.

The consequence of such a doctrine, as that a man could commit himself for any future publication, made without his privity, would be so wild and desperate, that it is unnecessary to do more than offer it to you in its true light.

But Carey has pinned the authority to a particular publication of the particular paper read in the Society. What question are you trying? are you trying the traverser for every possible publication which might have been sent to O'Donnell's paper; do you live in a country where such unlimited power is given to informers? Suppose Carey to have taken from O'Donnell's paper, a libel which Dr Drennan never saw—he is, by this doctrine, responsible—is it not too ridiculous? and does it not come to this, that Carey was tied down to publish that particular paper read in the Society, and no other; has he said then that it was the same paper which appeared in the *Dublin* Journal? where is the evidence that it was the same paper, and where is the guilt of Dr Drennan?

But, it will be said, by his declaration of an intent to publish it, he made himself answerable. Did he give it to O'Donnell to be published by him? or, to take a previous question, did O'Donnell publish it himself? has he said so? no such thing; but, what did he tell you? that any other printer might have published the paper produced, if he had had the materials; but it is highly probable that he printed it. What! is a man to be sent for two years to gaol, because you believe it *highly probable* that O'Donnell published this paper? Are you prepared by any impression whatsoever, so far to humble your minds, as to swear that McDonnell did publish this very paper? tho' the man himself cannot say so. Where is your honesty, or where is your common sense, if they can be *flattened* down into a verdict founded on nothing but your own credulity?

If Dr Drennan had given the paper to O'Donnell, the acts of the printer might derive credit from the original author; as it is, see how far this would be carrying constructive authority. What, my lord, is the act of the third person?—Is it the law that the act of a printer, with the witness Lestrange, should affect the traverser, who knew nothing of the transaction? The argument is that the delivery by McDonnell to Lestrange, was, no doubt, a publication by the traverser; but I say that nothing he does or says can affect Dr Drennan.

Suppose I were charged with committing murder, and that I had employed the crier of the court for the purpose; if he did the fact by my directions, he is guilty; but no concession of his can be evidence against me: So the publication of McDonnell, with the authority of Dr Drennan, might be evidence; but no declaration of McDonnell's can be evidence. The argument is that McDonnell admitted the fact, by giving the paper to the Stamp Officer; but was this admission on oath? Is what he said to a petty Officer of Stamps to be evidence against my client? But McDonnell does not recollect this transaction; he does not, on his oath, confirm the statement by Lestrange; and yet you are desired to take Lestrange's evidence of what McDonnell did. If you do, purposes may indeed be answered; and we have heard that there are many prosecutions in *petto*—many persons over whom the arm of the law is only suspended.

This may be policy, to keep the abandoned informer haunting the slumbers of the innocent man; but it is for you to consider, is such a time as this proper for it? In the present melancholy of the public mind, how far will it heal the grief which afflicts society? Or, will it not rather answer the immediate and selfish objects of those, whom a small gale may waft to that point, where the recollection of the country, and its situation, will never assail their ears?

But of the *probability* of this evidence, how shall I speak? What does it depend on? The integrity of the man who swears it. Do you think, gentlemen, that in every case an oath is a sufficient measure, to weigh down life and liberty, where a miscreant swears guilt against a man, must you convict him?

The declaration that the paper would appear in the Hibernian Journal stands on the single evidence of Carey; was he consistent with himself? If he did not appear to you upon that table a perjured man, believe every word he said. This man was under two prosecutions for this and another libel; this charge is to rest as well on his memory as his credit. He received a summons, signed by the Lord Chief Justice of Ireland!! do you believe, gentlemen, that Lord Clonmell's name was to it? Examine Mr Kemmis!

What is the answer? That he thought it was—he could not answer—he was sure it was. And this man, who comes to tell of words *spoken* two years ago, makes this silly mistake about the Chief Justice's name. Again—"Who are you?" I was under "prosecution—I was a member of the Society— I do not know whether I would have prosecuted or not, if they had kept their word." Three different things he swore as to my Lord's name. He did recollect—next, he did not—and, last of all, he could not tell. Does he not appear that kind of man, on whose evidence no man ought to be convicted. Scarce ever have I known a conviction on the mere evidence of an informer; but see what motives this man has—under prosecution for the same crime, he has not only his own safety to consult, but the most avowed and rancorous malice to Dr Drennan; he swore he had none. Did you not hear of his declaration of vengenance! A gentleman comes and swears that he said he thought it no crime to assassinate Drennan, for a refusal to support him under a criminal prosecution—to support the man who proposed to the society to arm against the government.

I asked him why he proposed this?—merely to try character. Was he himself sincere?—he was! he was perfectly sincere; and yet it was a mere fetch to try character!

As to the influence of his situation on his evidence, what did he say?; he was not sure of a pardon, but he hoped for one. If you give credit to this man, you make a fine harvest for informers; a fine opportunity you give to every ruffian in society; and you may go home in the comfortable conviction that it is far from impossible that the next attack shall be on yourselves; and if your wives are superstitious, or your children undutiful, you may have them going to fortune-tellers to enquire "when Mr Carey shall be unmuzzled against you."

So far as Bell's testimony was appealed to, he contradicted Carey. He did not believe that the words of address stood any part of the paper read, and no human being has given evidence of the general susbtance. Bell contradicted him again; for he said there were no orders made to print it in any paper; and what did Wright say?—That it was after the publication in the Hibernian Journal that Carey complained to him of having been neglected; and asked should he publish the paper? How shall I publish it? says he, the Evening Post is nonsense; says Wright, take it from the Hibernian Journal. Here is the positive oath of this unimpeached witness contradicting Carey's evidence. Unfortunate—perjured man—he makes a complaint that he received no instructions; he complains of the whole society. Gentlemen, do you believe Wright?

But there is a way in which you may get out of this. It will be said, "God forbid, that a man should not perjure himself in one or two little points, and tell truth in the whole;" an old woman may say that oaths are but wind, he might tell truth at other times. Did you ever, gentlemen, hear of a point in which a perjured witness might be believed? Yes, there is one—when he says he is perjured. The principle is as strong in our hearts as if it had been written by the finger of that God who said, *thou shalt not bear false witness.* The law of the country has said that the man, once convicted of false swearing, shall not a second time contaminate the walls of a court of justice; and it is the very essence of a jury that if a man appears (though not yet marked out by the law as a perjurer) to have foiled his nature by the deliberate commission of this crime, that moment his credit shall cease with the jury; his evidence shall be blotted from their minds, and leave no trace but horror and indignation.

I feel the hardship of their situation when grave and learned men are brought forward to support such a prosecution—I have great respect for them, for some of them I have had it from my boyish days, but this respect does not prevent my saying that, as officers of state, their private worth is not to weigh with you; it is for their credit to deceive you; they have no power to control a prosecution; if one is commanded they must carry it on; and when they talk of their character, what do they say? "If the evidence is insufficient, take a little of our dignity to eke it out." What their feelings are, is nothing to you, gentlemen; they may have feelings of another kind to compensate for them.

But while I lament this, I will show that your sympathy is not called forth for nothing. Why do we hear such expressions as these? "I speak under the authority of a former jury;" has that verdict been given in evidence? no; could it govern you if it had? no. Here you see the necessity of an appeal to official dignity. We heard of clubs formed in this city, we had no evidence of them that their object was to separate the countries,—does this appear? To pull the king from his throne—what can I say, but "how does this appear?;" not a word of it has been proved; and here let me mention the impolicy of such expressions, and say that the frequent recital of such circumstances will rather reconcile profligate minds to them than deter them.

As to the Society of United Irishmen, I have had the misfortune, from my strong reprobation of their conduct, to incur much contumelious animadversion; but where is their desperate purpose to be found? Is it in the rejection of Carey's proposal to arm? Does this show their design to pull the king from the throne, or to separate the countries?—But it comes down to the *horrible blasphemy* of reviling the Police. To make their case more hideous and more aggravated, you are told of their blaspheming the *sanctified* Police—the *holy, prudent and oeconomical* Police.

Did they suppose that they were addressing the liquorish loyalty of a guzzling corporation? Or do you suppose, gentlemen, that there is a collation of *custards* prepared for you when you leave the jury box, when they wished to excite your compassion for the *abused* Police? But it is said that they not only attack existing establishments, but fully the character of the *unborn* Militia; that they hurl their shafts against what was to be raised the next year. "So, *Gossip*," says the flatterer to *Timon*. "What," says he, "I did not know you had children;"—"nay, but I will marry shortly, and my first child shall be called Timon, and then we shall be gossips." So this *wizard*, Drennan, found out that a Militia was to be raised the next year; and that he not only abused the *Corporation*, but the Police and the Militia.

Do they think you are such buzzards—such blind creatures—do they think you are only fit to go to school—or rather to go no where that one part would be punished for no other reason than its exact similarity to the other?

I protest I have been eighteen years at this bar, and never until this last year have I seen such witnesses supporting charges of this kind with such abandoned profligacy. In one case, where men were on their trial for their lives, I felt myself involuntarily shrinking under your lordship's protection from the miscreant who leaped upon the table and announced himself a witness. I hoped the practice would have remained

105

in those distant parts of the country where it began, but I am disappointed; I see the period fast approaching, when a man shall be judged before he is tried—when the advocate shall be libelled for discharging his duty to his client; that night of human nature, when a man shall be hunted down, not because he is a criminal, but because he is obnoxious.

Punish a man in the situation of Dr Drennan, and what do you do? what will become of the liberty of the press? you will have newspapers filled with the drowsy adulations of some persons who want benefices, or commissions in the revenue, or commissions in the army; here and there, indeed, you may chance to see a paragraph of this kind—

"Yesterday came on to be tried, for the publication of a seditious libel, Dr William Drennan. The great law-officer of the crown stated the case in the most candid and temperate manner. During his speech every man in court was in an agony of horror; the gentlemen of the jury—many of them from the rotation-office—were all staunch whigs, and friends to government. Mr Carey came on the table, and declared that he had no malice against the traverser; and most honourably denied the assertion in his next breath. It was proved much to his honour that he had declared his intention to assassinate the traverser. The jury listened with great attention. Mr Curran, with his usual ability, defended the traverser;"—for he must have been ably defended. *"Dr Wright was produced, a bloody minded United Irishman—he declared, he could not say but that Doctor Drennan was the author of the libel; and that the types were very like each other in the face. An able speech was made in reply by his Majesty's Prime Serjeant. He said, with the utmost propriety, that the jury knew little of him, if they supposed him to prosecute without a perfect conviction of the traverser's guilt, that Mr Curran's great abilities had been spent in jests on the subject; that the perjuries were mere little inconsistencies, the gentleman having much on his mind. He made many pertinent observations on the aspersions thrown out on the corporation of Dublin.*

"Here Mr Curran interposed, and assured him he intended no such aspersions. The Prime Serjeant declared, he thought he had heard them. That as to the Police, they were a most honourable body of men; that a number of looking glasses, and other articles of furniture, were highly necessary for them; and as to the militia, the attack on that was abominable, for that it was shameful to asperse a body intended to be raised by government next year.

"The Jury—a most worshipful, worthy jury, retired for a few minutes, and returned with a verdict of GUILTY, much to the satisfaction of the public."

To this sort of language will you reduce the freedom of public discussion, by a conviction of the traverser; and if the liberty of the press is destroyed for a supposed abuse, this is the kind of discussion you will have.

PRIME SERJEANT. Gentlemen of the jury, notwithstanding what you have just heard from the traverser's counsel, I feel no apprehension on my mind that you will act otherwise than what belongs to justice. I trust that you will discharge your duty as becomes men, I have little fear that you will be terrified by the excommunication which has been denounced against you, if you believe the traverser guilty of this charge; and I am confident that "*buzzards*" and "*dunces*," as you are—upon your oaths, you will do right.

There are in this case two simple questions: Is the paper a libel? and did Dr Drennan publish it? Was it intended to excite and diffuse, among the king's subjects, jealousies, discontents, and suspicions of our lord the king and his government, and disaffection and disloyalty to his person—to raise seditions and tumults, to draw the government into disgrace, and incite the king's subjects to alter the constitution by force? If you cannot answer in the affirmative to every one of these questions, I shall subscribe to his acquittal—if you think it is not a most mischievous libel. But if you believe it is so, and that he is guilty—if any consideration shall weigh with you against the truth, you will stand committed to this country for all the mischiefs which may follow.

The first question to be considered is the publication; upon this I shall not dwell long, for I contend for it, that the publication by the traverser's means, in the Hibernian Journal, was a publication by him. See what the evidence is? Two witnesses on the part of the prosecution; and one on the part of the traverser, agree as to the material circumstances of the publication.—Carey, Bell, and Wright, all concur that there was a meeting; that Dr Drennan was the chairman; that he read the address paragraph by paragraph; that alterations were made in it on the report of the committee; that the question was put from the chair, and that it was agreed to by the Society.

Carey has sworn to his order to publish it; and no attempt was made on the part of the traverser to controvert that order; it was ordered to be printed in three different newspapers.—

The earliest days on which it could be published were the day after in the Evening Post, and in the Hibernian Journal, of the Monday ensuing; the meeting was on the Friday evening. The traverser, by his direction to copy the Hibernian Journal, made that paper his original publication.

So far as I can form a judgment, Mr Carey's conduct does not deserve the reprobation it has met with; the man was forced, not on the examination for the crown, but on that for the traverser, to go into an explanation of the motives and intentions of this society; it was then you heard of their design of urging the people to take arms against the——

MR CURRAN. I beg leave to state that what Carey mentioned was that an attempt was made to call on the Society to take arms; not the people at large.

PRIME SERJEANT. You heard the evidence, gentlemen, and recollect it; but I mention this only to show the delicacy of Carey, in recollecting those circumstances, even when he was compelled (by the society's deserting him) to an act of duty; only when he was abandoned by them, he began to think that Drennan, as the prime cause, and not himself, a mere instrument, should go to gaol for this libel.

Having then fixed the authority of the traverser, as to the original in the Hibernian Journal, the next piece of evidence is Lestrange's, who proves that he got the paper from McDonnell; McDonnell swears that he never gave one which was not printed at his office; here then you have the paper referred to as the original, proved by this chain of evidence; and if Carey's object had been to obtain the traverser's conviction by perjury, what was easier, or less likely to be contradicted, than to have sworn that he bought this very paper at McDonnell's shop, or that he had brought the paper to Drennan, who had given specific directions to have it printed; but, on the contrary, he is peculiarly delicate in his evidence, and tells you fairly that the paper from which he published was destroyed in the usual course of printing; he confessed fairly that he had a resentment to Drennan, and he would not be a man if he had not a manly resentment against him; but he has disclaimed all malice, for malice does not belong to manly resentment.

These appear the leading circumstances attending the publication; and if you are satisfied that the publication in the Hibernian Journal was made by his direction and approbation, you cannot have any doubt on your minds that the traverser published this paper. The next question is that of libel or not? In considering this, I shall decline travelling minutely through the different paragraphs of this libel; I shall merely observe on its general tendency.

It commences with a plausible and imposing title of a society, from whose title no can could suppose to find a paper pregnant with sedition and disorder proceed—*the Society of United Irishmen.*

From the first sentence you have the traverser's own opinion as to the state of the country: He tells you (if he is author) that "from the proclamation which has been issued, it is natural to apprehend danger at home and abroad;" this was the situation of the country when this manifesto issued. He then proceeds to tell you that the proclamation has excited "rumours and whispers," and is calculated to "shake the public credit;" and, again, to excite the fears of "old man, women and children."

I shall only observe this was in consequence of a proclamation, by which certain men, who had avowed an intention of arraying themselves against the government, were prohibited from arming. They "will cry aloud amidst the storm raised by the witchcraft of this proclamation;" a proclamation which every man who regards the country must reverence, and the merit of advising which, every man who could claim it has been so desirous of sharing, as to pilfer it from the original movers; are such expressions as these calculated to reconcile to the goverment, and to the laws, those who were so protected by them?

This paper then calls on the Volunteers to arm—for what purpose?—the next sentence will tell you. The constituted authorities are likely to oppose their proceedings; another body must therefore be opposed to them. "A notorious Police." My learned friend is little acquainted with the estimation in which the Police is held in the counties where it is established; when he ridicules them, he little knows of what additional value property is in those countries which have them, and how highly their presence is desired by those who have them not. The great constitutional army—the Militia—is next exposed to odium—fatal odium—! Many have been the unhappy wretches who have sacrificed their lives to the too successful insinuations of this libel. How could it be otherwise, when just before the establishment of that Militia, such a libel as this was sent through the country, to brand it even in embryo.

At the same moment that they tell you there is danger abroad and at home, the army, whose tried fidelity must certainly have made them obnoxious to this society, the army are told, that "the defence of their country is too honourable a trust for mercenaries." Happy would it have been for the country to have had a more numerous army, if this paper had succeeded according to the wish of its author; for more would have been necessary, if the "witchcraft" of "this proclamation" had not frighted those disturbers into their senses. See how strongly the attack is directed against the powers supporting the government—the Volunteers are called "to stand to their arms"—the Police and Militia "are calculated to disturb good order,"—the constitution is dead, and can only revive "by a military array of Volunteers;"—and, to crown all, the soldiery are told, "that seduction made them soldiers."—By a dash of the pen, the whole army is to be disbanded; they are called on to show their resentment of that seduction which was practised on them; and by a society which has no authority, but "that derived from reason,"—or, in other words, from publications inflammatory and seditious as this is.

The libel then *commands* government to "anticipate revolution, by a well timed reform."—Is this language plain enough?—does it require explanation? The armed Volunteers are next called on, to attend a convention to assemble at Dungannon—for what purpose?—for the purpose of publishing their manifestoes at the point of the bayonet.

Here follows some of their moderation—"We offer only a sketch"—answer us with arms in your hands—attend our convention—and we will then submit our general address.—

"Would remain unrepresented,"—If there was not another line in this paper, this would support all the charges in the indictment. The man who tells the people they are unrepresented is an incendiary of the most dangerous nature; what is it but to say, you have no law—no constitution.

The next sentence,—"How many nations have gotten the start of Ireland?" I can hardly suppose, but that I must suppose—was intended to reprobate us being behind France in the race of blood and horror; I cannot suppose my countrymen are such *buzzards* as to be abashed at such their inactivity.

It is for you to consider whether this paper be mischievous, as I have alleged it to be; it lay on the traverser to prove either that (if he did publish it) he did it innocently, or without the intentions with which he is charged.

I have trespassed too long on you, gentlemen; I shall, therefore, only say, that we rest our case on the second count of the indictment.

Mr Emmett rose to set the Prime Serjeant right, as to one fact; he had supposed the publication of the Hibernian Journal to have been prior to that of the Star, but by Wright's evidence it appeared that the Star was published without the paper, on the Saturday after, the same evening on which it appeared in the Evening Post, and that the Hibernian Journal was published on Monday, and the conversation with Wright was on Tuesday.

ATTORNEY GENERAL. The direction to Carey was, that it should be taken from the Hibernian Journal, which could not be done till that paper was published.

THE COURT *requested some of the counsel on each side to remain in court while they were charging the jury.*

EARL CLONMELL. Gentlemen of the Jury, before I go into the consideration of this case, which has occupied the whole day, I think it necessary to point out to you the extent of your duty, as prescribed in a late statute, by which it is declared and enacted "that on the trial of any indictment or information," this is an indictment, gentlemen—"the jury may give a general verdict of guilty or not guilty, upon the whole matter in issue, and shall not be required or directed by the court or judge, before whom such indictment or information shall be tried, to find the defendant or defendants guilty, merely on the proof of the publication, by such defendants of the paper charged to be a libel, and of the sense ascribed to the same, in such indictment or information." 33 Geo. 3. c. 63. s.1.

In this case an issue is joined between the king and the traverser; you are the jury, and are to give your verdict on the whole matter in issue.

I state this the rather in this case—both because I think it necessary, that the law should be universally understood—and because in this particular case, the question to be tried is more particularly for your consideration than it generally happens to be in most other cases of libels.

This indictment which you have so often heard read, both from the Clerk, and the gentlemen of the bar, contains nine *counts*—which means nine different modes of making the charge; eight of these have been abandoned, and the proof directed only to the second charge; and to that you are to apply your attention pointedly. In this count then the grand jury have found that "William Drennan, Doctor of Physic, maliciously, designing, and intending dangerous and seditious tumults, to raise, to draw government into disgrace, to excite the king's subjects to attempt with force and violence, and with arms, to make alterations in the government, state and constitution of this country, to excite the people to tumult and anarchy, and to over-awe the legislature by an armed force, &c." did on a certain day publish this paper in the Hibernian Journal or Chronicle of Liberty.

[*Here Mr Justice Downes hinted something to the Chief Justice.*]

My brother Downes is obliging enough to mention, that the Attorney General relied upon the eighth count also for a general publication; the second charges it in the Hibernian Journal; this charges it generally, without naming any paper; of course, if the first count be supported by evidence, the second must also stand. The reason I confined my observation to the second was because I thought the Prime Serjeant had pretty explicitly given up all the rest.

To support this charge, William Paulet Carey was produced.

Carey's paper was not offered in evidence, and should be therefore thrown out of your recollection.

[Here his Lordship recited Carey's evidence.]

He swore "that he received a notice—that the Chief Justice's name was to it;" this was sufficiently exposed by Mr Curran. There could have been no such notice—it must have been an absurd falsehood. He swears, "that he was sincere in his proposal to arm;" and again he tells you, "it was to try the sincerity of others." He cannot recollect the words of address." (The title.)

He attributed whatever inconsistency he might have shown, to his having been "baited" by Mr Curran. This is the apology he made for himself.

So much has been said, by way of observation on this paper, that I shall offer very little, especially as it is on the degree of credit which you give to this witness, your verdict must in a great measure stand. All that could be said to impeach that credit has been strongly put by Mr Curran, and it remains with you to judge of it. It has been endeavoured to make him appear a man acting under the influence and expectation of a pardon. It has been observed that he said, "he did not know whether he would have given up Drennan or not;" and afterwards, "if he had been supported, he would not have done so." These points have been made, to show that he did not act under the influence of truth. His apology still was, that he had been so baited by questions from counsel.—This is all for your consideration.

The next witness was McDonnell. No paper was read out of his book—I shall not, therefore, dwell on it. He said he found an address at his house on his return home on a Sunday. This circumstance is worthy your recollection.

Lestrange was then produced, and he swears positively to some facts: That he got an Hibernian Journal, dated the 17th of December, 1792, from McDonnell; and, for the purpose of connecting the fact of publication with that of identity, McDonnell swears that he never delivered to any one, as his paper, one not printed by him. I suppose this was to exclude the idea of another paper of that name being circulated or printed by any other person. He swears that he charged the publication to the United Irishmen.

Whitaker was next produced; in short he said nothing. The paper was then read, in which the libel complained of in the indictment appears.

Mr Bell said, [*here his lordship recited Bell's evidence.*]

MR EMMETT. My lord, I beg leave to remind your lordship that Bell also said he did not recollect any resolution for publishing this address in any paper.

MR JUSTICE DOWNES. Only in answer to a general question, no particular resolution was described to bring it to his recollection.

EARL CLONMELL. Traynor is next produced; he tells you that Carey declared, "he would think it no crime to assassinate Drennan, who had expelled him, and ruined his peace of mind." This has been properly dwelt on; but it goes also to confirm what Carey himself said, that he was angry with the traverser; that he wrote him a letter to say so, and (as he insinuated very strongly) to challenge him to fight him. Wooloughan is the next witness; he shows Carey's mortification and resentment; which Carey acknowledges himself. Wright swears positively that Carey told him he had no instructions as to this publication, and that he expressed his displeasure at that circumstance, saying he was ill-used, that he was not at that time determined whence to take it, so that if you believe Wright, he contradicts Carey's oath, when he told you he had directions from Drennan; and if Wright is to be believed, this shows you that what Carey said was not

115

true. Upon the whole, it is said at the bar, that you have the oaths of three uncontradicted witnesses, to prove that there was such a meeting on the 14th of December; that the traverser was chairman of it, that a question was put by him on an address; that it was agreed to, and ordered to be published.

Mr Emmett here suggested to his lordship, that he had understood Bell's evidence differently.

Earl Clonmell read his notes over again, and the other Judges having read from their notes the evidence, it appeared perfectly to correspond; the foreman of the jury also read his notes, which coincided with his lordship's.

MR EMMETT. I did not understand it so; but I submit to your lordships.

EARL CLONMELL. This was the evidence as I took it; my brothers have been so good as to compare with me; I am always glad of the assistance of the bar; I never consider such as interruption, especially when it comes in the gentleman-like way in which this was given.

Gentlemen of the Jury, there are three questions for your consideration; one which the act declares you have a right to consider, whether this is a libel or not; indeed I might say there are four questions, I had almost overlooked one which is of small consequence, whether the innuendoes are well filled up, that is, whether "this city" means the city of Dublin, and so forth.

But the three main questions for you are, first, whether the paper deserves the appellations and attributes annexed to by the indictment.

Secondly. Whether it was published by the traverser, or by his means, or whether he caused it to be published; and thirdly, whether if he did so, it was with the intentions ascribed to him by the indictment.

As to the first question, I am bound to tell you my opinion, as I am in all criminal cases; and I have no hesitation in my mind to declare that this paper is a wicked and seditious libel, deserving all the appellations in the indictment, and in this I am desired to anticipate my brothers, by saying that they perfectly concur in this opinion. The next is, whether you believe it to have been published by the traverser; but before I go into this, I again will mention my decided opinion, that this is not a paper of discussion, but of stimulation to arms; and it is from my being so perfectly clear that I do not go into it paragraph by paragraph; its tendency appears to me to be, to overturn the constitution; to overwhelm the legislature; to establish a new and despotic power, to carry those objects by arms—to destroy the constitution by force— to asperse the existing government—to stimulate the minds of the people at large, and to establish by force and arms a new system of representation.

But all this avails nothing against the traverser, if you do not believe he was the publisher of this paper; and this must stand upon a question of fact, of which you are the sole judges. If you believe Carey, Drennan ordered him to publish this libel and referred him to the Hibernian Journal as the model from which to copy. "You will find," says he, "the address which I have moved this night, in the Hibernian Journal of next Monday." This question then turns upon Carey's credit, for no other witness has sworn to these instructions of Drennan to Carey, and you have Wright's testimony in contradiction, telling you that Carey on the Tuesday after complained of want of instruction.

It appears by uncontroverted evidence that an address was moved, that a question was put on it while the traverser was in the chair, and the paper complained of appears in the Hibernian Journal next ensuing; so far this corresponds with Carey's evidence, and his credit depends entirely upon you. Lestrange produces the Hibernian Journal in question, he swears he got it from McDonnell, who swears that he never did give a paper as the Hibernian Journal which he did not publish, so that the publication of Monday appears, and

117

contains the libel, but, gentlemen, if you do not believe that Carey received those instructions, I think you ought to acquit the traverser, for this is the only way in which the thing is brought home to him—if you believe that he did give those directions, and caused the libel to be published in the Hibernian Journal, connecting all this with his motion in the Society, it attaches guilt to him so far as to the question of publication, and if you believe this, and are also of opinion that this paper is of the tendency which I think it is, there remains but one question more upon which you can hesitate to find him guilty.

This leads us to the question of *intention*. See how the circumstances stand as to his intentions—it is sworn that he put the question on this address—that he read it deliberately—that he caused it to be published—and here let me caution you from supposing that I am saying that this is the same address; the only foundation you have for that is, (if you believe Carey) the direction to him—"you will find *this* in the Hibernian Journal—take yours from it."

If then, I say, you believe that he caused the publication of the address which you have heard, I have little difficulty in saying that his having read it is strong evidence to show that he knew what its meaning and intentions were.

If you believe that he published this paper—that it is a libel—and that he knew it to be so—you will find him guilty on the first and eighth counts.

If you do not believe that this is a libel—or that it was not published by Dr Drennan's means, or that he did it by any accident, innocently; but it is no excuse that he thought it a good measure—for if that defence were allowed, it would aid the vilest man in society; a man might think it advantageous to make a massacre to produce a certain purpose—he might commit murder to rid society of a person he thought mischievous; it is an excuse which might be offered for every crime. If then, you believe that he knew and understood the meaning of that paper, it comes up to my idea of the ground of guilt in this last point.

I have thus stated the situations in which you should convict, or acquit. I have only to add, that if your minds should be in a state of struggling suspense—you ought to lean in favour of acquittal.

MR JUSTICE DOWNES. Gentlemen of the jury, it is totally unnecessary for me to trouble you with any particular observations, after what you have heard from his lordship; I entirely agree with him that this is a libel; and if upon the grounds stated to you, you shall be of opinion that the traverser did publish it, you ought in my mind to find him guilty.

MR JUSTICE CHAMBERLAIN. I have no hesitation in saying that I think this is a libel of the most dangerous and treasonable nature I ever met with; it is a direct invitation to the Volunteers to overturn the constitution by a convention, and an armed force; and however legal it may be to seek a reform by constitutional means, yet to call upon the people to do so with arms is in my mind highly seditious; and as such I consider this a libel, that is however a question for you to consider.

As to all the other parts of this case, they are mere matters of fact unmixed with law. The question of publication in my opinion depends on Carey's testimony of the directions given to him by the traverser, "to take the address from the Hibernian Journal of the next Monday;" if you disbelieve him in that particular, there is no evidence to convict; much has been said of Carey's situation; he comes, no doubt, in the nature of an accomplice, but his credit is a question for you only, and if you disbelieve him in the material part, or doubt, still more if you think he told a deliberate falsehood, you ought to acquit the traverser.

The Jury retired at ten o'clock; about a quarter past eleven a verdict being announced, and the usual form of calling the jury,

119

&c. gone through, the officer of the Court asked, "Is the traverser guilty of the first count in the indictment or not?" Not guilty was scarcely pronounced by the Foreman, when the court rung with indecent and vociferous plaudits, huzzaing, clapping of hands, and throwing up of hats; which continuing for some time, the Foreman returned to the room with some of the jury. One of the judges ordered the jury to be called, and desired they might give in their verdict. On the Foreman's return to the box, the clamour having somewhat ceased, he addressed the court:

"My lords, as I consider this a trial of the first importance to the peace of the country, and the happiness of society, I must conceive such indecent conduct as we have experienced, to bespeak a spreading pernicious spirit, which by an exertion of power, ought to be suppressed. For my own part, timidity has no influence on my mind—I act without fear—I despise the resentment, and disregard the approbation of an unruly and seditious rabble; and I can assure them they have no cause for exultation in meeting favour from the jury; for they regret at seeing a criminal they cannot reach, and guilt which they cannot punish."

The other counts were then severally put to the jury, and a verdict of NOT GUILTY, received upon all.

In the course of the tumult in the outer hall one of the High Sheriffs (Mr Giffard) selected an opulent citizen (Mr S. Gardiner of Church Street), who appeared an active disturber. Complaint was made to the Court next day by the Sheriff, and a rule put upon Gardiner to show cause why an attachment should not issue against him for the contempt; whereupon he filed an affidavit, in which he relied much upon the court's having been, at the time of his apprehension, adjourned. Counsel was heard for him; but the court was pleased to make the rule absolute for attaching him.

THE END

INTENDED DEFENCE,

ON A TRIAL FOR SEDITION, IN THE YEAR 1794

MY LORDS,

It was not my intention, until very lately, to have intruded on your time with any vindication or exculpation of myself, but to have resigned the whole of this business to the ability of my council, the justice of the jury, and the large discretion of the court; remaining, myself, in the silence of self-approving conscience, satisfied with the simple sincerity expressed in two words—not guilty. Yet, as this silence is ambiguous, except to God and my own conscience, and may be misinterpreted by enemies, and even by friends, as proceeding from various motives, independent of the real one, which is, in truth, the calm conviction of my own innocence, I shall, therefore, entreat your permission, my Lords, to make a few observations; and I take the liberty of reading them, from a fear of saying anything irregular or unpremeditated, and from a diffidence, which a conscious want of abilities, and the novelty of my present situation, naturally inspire; as I have never in the course of my life, more than twice or thrice, entered a court of justice.

It is certain, that the very essence and pith of all criminality consists in the *intention*. It is the will, intention, or mind, with which the thing is done, that ought to be respected as constituting the guilt; for one may fall into error, but no error, in itself, deserves punishment; and a man may be a mistaken zealot, without being at the same time a seditious disturber of the public peace. Allowing the paper to be in its nature libellous, the libellous or seditious intention remains to be proved; and this inward and invisible intention is to be collected and deduced from outward acts, and from concomitant circumstances. As in a written paper, it is not merely one or two imprudent or incautious expressions which should make it be condemned, as, in the whole, a seditious libel, without an impartial consideration and comparison of the text and context taken together—so, if a person be accused of having authorized such a publication, with an intention to disturb the public peace, the proof of that intention ought not to rest on the consideration of a single isolated action, supposing it to *be* ascertained, but on a fair comparison of what may be called the *context* of that man's life; on its disagreement, or coincidence, with the subject matter of the accusation.

This, therefore, must be my reason and my apology for presuming to speak of myself; and as it is necessary to prove, that in speech, in writing, or in action, the only means of revealing the hidden heart, I have been a man the most unlikely to form designs of disturbing the public peace; (for what, indeed, would become of such an atom as me, in the storm of civil commotion?) and that all my external conduct has branched from the root of a single principle infixed in my heart, agitating its every pulse, and constituting a part of its very existence—an enthusiastic desire for an equal representation of all my countrymen in their own House of Parliament, with which I conceive public morals, public happiness, and public peace, are most intimately connected. Were I not convinced, that nothing very great or very good was ever effectuated without a portion of enthusiasm, and that such a passionate prepossession in favour of a good principle, ought to be freely pardoned, or with pity punished, I should have used the term enthusiastic with some apprehension of ridicule, at a time when to behave disinterestedly, wears an appearance of insanity; and to cleave to principles, instead of being complimented as preserving integrity, is a mark of a man being a Jacobin, a madman, or a fool.

A jury is chosen from the vicinage, that an acquaintance with the merits of the case, and the characters of those concerned, may produce perfect justice from perfect knowledge; but still they are also in the vicinage, I may say the contact of much party prejudice; and elevated as they are, and sitting apart amidst the sanctity of a court of justice, the most holy place upon earth, next to the temple of God, they are still immersed in the foul air of this low world. The same extravagance of a good principle, which may have led the author of that address, in the fervour of the mind, beyond the line of discretion, might lead *them*, in the desire, equally zealous, of keeping down what has been supposed a dangerous faction, to act, in the present instance, rather from a vague, general, and indiscriminate condemnation of certain principles, than from a calm and impartial scrutiny of the character and conduct of the individual before them. They ought to rise so far above the atmosphere of party, as to look down from the serenity of a clear judgment, and with the sympathy of humanity; to select the particular case; to consider it under all its relations of character, of times, and of circumstances; for, without such discrimination, the office of a jury, in periods like the present, when men and the times are so out of temper, would resemble the movement of a great machine, blind and exceptionless—not a body of men who can pause, and make those allowances for others, which in similar situations they should wish to be made for themselves.

They ought not to reason, in my case, or in any other, from the general objection, to the individual instance; from the condemnation of the party, to that of the person, without estimating fairly different gradations, and making grounds of exception, though, on the whole, their principles may have led them to reprobate and condemn. Round numbers, and general appellations, are equally exaggerating and to be distrusted. Men are generally better than their sect, and the

123

partisan than the party. The conscience of the jury ought to ask itself, how far their dislike of my political principles, how far the desire to put down a party, and how far many other circumstances, collateral and accidental, may tend to bias and seduce their judgment respecting the individual case; and if my life, in the review which is their duty to make of it, be an innocent life, that must be a reason for distrusting their judgment, on any single act of it being seditious; as that judgment may proceed from the misconception of my intention, seen through the medium of certain political antipathies. The whole of a paper should be taken into consideration, to ground the judgment of it as a libel; and the conclusion of a seditious intention should be drawn from looking at the whole life.

I am the son of an honest man; a minister of that gospel which breathes peace and goodwill among men; a Protestant Dissenting minister, in the town of Belfast; who[se] spirit I am accustomed to look up, in every trying situation, as my mediator and intercessor with Heaven. He was the friend and associate of good, I may say, great men; of Abernethy, of Bruce, of Duchal, and of Hucheson; and his character of mild and tender benevolence is still remembered by many in the North of Ireland, and by not a few in this city.

I may be imprudent in mentioning, that he was, and that I glory to be, a Protestant Dissenter, obnoxious as this appellation is at present, in both countries; but my future life would appear to me one continued lie, were I not on this occasion to profess myself one of that division of Protestants who regard no authority on earth, in matters of religion, save the words and the works of its author, and whose fundamental principle it is that every person has a right, and in proportion to his abilities, is under an obligation, to judge for himself in matters of religion; a right, subservient to God alone, not a favour to be derived from the gratuitous lenity of government; a right, the resignation of which produces slavery on the one hand, persecution on the other; and of consequence that disturbance of the public peace, which has so much, and so long distinguished the Christian world.

Such religious principles, founded as they are on the right of private judgment, to be accounted as sacred in others as in ourselves, naturally produce that independence of mind, which is the buckler of political as well as private virtue, and has made the Protestant Dissenters, in all critical times, the active defenders and guardians of the British constitution; and to the best of fathers, the best of religions, and the best, as I think, of persuasions included in that religion, am I indebted for that veneration of the rights of mankind, which I find to be the true source of personal happiness, because the violation of any right must be the transgression of a duty, and so far must make a man miserable. From the earliest of my school-boy days, from the delightful hours in which I voyaged with the patient, persevering Ulysses, and made *his* country the Ithaca of my wishes, in which I panted through the Greek and Roman story; from those days, the love of my country has been in my breast, not merely a classical image, or a cold principle, but an animating spring of action; and surely, our ancient poets, orators, and historians, would have been long ago placed by some inquisitorial committee in a political "index expurgatorius," and prohibited from the use of youth, were it not hoped, that the bustle of a selfish world would soon brush off such childish ideas, and that the prudence, and caution, and moderation of a premature old age, would keep down, even in manhood, the propensities of nature, and the instinct of liberty.

I have heard that the first address which Sir Robert Walpole (he who deflowered the British constitution) was accustomed to make to the young men who were sent for to his closet, was, "Well, sir, are you really resolved to continue an old Roman?" and on hearing it, I have cursed the public bawd, whose aim it was to blast the blossoming virtues of the heart; and have blessed my own good fortune, that education, habit, small ability, and simple integrity, would always shield me from such seducing connections.

In the year 1778, when the people of Ireland took up arms through necessity, but through public spirit retained them: when the public peace was undisturbed, because the people were armed; when common danger united all ranks whom the feeling of a common country could not unite before, I entered, with ardent zeal, and feeble frame, into the first Volunteer association made in this kingdom, and was among the first and among the last in that ever memorable institution which saved the island from invasion, secured domestic tranquillity, advanced civil liberty, laid the foundation of national independence, and by their liberal resolutions, showed toleration to be but a mitigated persecution; and taught administration a lesson, which they were soon after obliged to put into practice, viz. that the surest way of guarding the constitution, is to interest as many of all descriptions of religion as is possible, in its preservation. Indeed, I associated everything great and good, everything most auspicious to the hopes, most connected with the best interests of the country, to an institution which raised every man in it to a higher value, and I wished it to be perpetual, with an ardour which he that has been a Volunteer might imagine would suggest such an address (as is the present subject of prosecution), on the supposed extinction of that body, and which he that has not felt, might excuse in an enthusiastic, but not ill-intentioned mind.

From the year 1778 to that of 1782, I observed such a line of conduct as might be expected from one who has ever most justly looked on himself most humbly as an individual, but most proudly as an Irishman; and, as an Irishman, I added one particle to that mass of public spirit which then asserted the exclusive rights, and legislative competency of this imperial island; its distinct dominion, and independent parliament: and I was one of the millions who *then* thought that the truest way of honouring Britain for renouncing her assumption of right, was to proceed in reforming every *internal* abuse that corrupted our constitution. I then thought, and I ever will think, that a more equal representation of the people, was absolutely necessary for their freedom, their virtue, their happiness, and their *peace*; and by exerting myself in my little sphere, by rallying all the powers I possessed round this central point, I thought that I was practising the doctrine of him who went about doing good continually to the poor people, himself poor and lowly; and that I was copying the example of a father who felt for all that lived, particularly for the living mass of humanity.

I thought that the truest way of promoting civil war, was to put the people out of conceit with the constitution, by hearing always of its perfections, and feeling only its abuses, until they might come to confound the excellencies of the government with the errors of its mal-administration; and that the truest way for promoting peace was, as in the case of the Volunteers, to arm the people for their liberties, so now, to arm them—with their rights, which is the first step in giving them a knowledge of their duties: for until they enjoy the one, they will remain ignorant of the other, and the exclusion which first made, will support the incapacity. The enjoyment of rights implies the performance of duties; and the unequal distribution of the former prevents the discharge of the latter; so that the freedom of the public is necessarily connected with their virtue as well as their happiness. An arbitrary, irregular, and undetermined subordination, not only checks and destroys industry, but is a provocative on the one part to every excess which is natural to the abuse of power without right; and on the other part, to those crimes, and that disturbance of the public peace, which the hopelessness of redressing their wrongs begets in ferocious and savage natures: and thus, to the corruptions of our constitution are traceable all the crime as well as misery of *our* civil society. I thought I should become an accessary in that crime, as well as a promoter of that misery, if I did not act as zealous advocate for a reform in parliament; and, as such, fervently desire, that the Volunteers should retain the possession of those arms which are the prime distinction of freemen; that this energetic establishment, arising from the innate vigour of the citizens, should perpetually exist, as being necessarily connected with that public spirit, in which alone I saw reason to hope for ultimate attainment of the great object—an adequate and impartial representation.

As my principles in religion were brought from nature and the New Testament, and as my reasons for being a Protestant Dissenter were early drawn from a book named "The Dissenting Gentleman's Answer to White;" and afterwards from Blackburne, Furneaux, Priestley, and Price; so my prime authority in politics was "Locke's Essay on Government;" and my authorities for the justice, the expediency, and the necessity of a parliamentary reform, were drawn from the general, I may say, the universal opinion of the deepest reasoners, the most splendid orators, and the best men; from the petitions of twenty-eight out of thirty-two counties in Ireland; from the concurrent opinion of two meetings, the nature and name of which are now under legal interdiction, the one a delegation of citizen-soldiers, sanctioned by Lord Charlemont, the other a delegation purely civil, where Mr Sharman presided, both equally inefficacious; from the authorities of persons, in other respects most opposite; from Flood and Grattan; from Fox and Pitt; from the first peers, and the lowest peasants; from the early principles of Richmond, and the purer practice of Burke. At this flame I lighted my taper; it illumined my understanding, warmed my heart, and influenced my conduct; and from 1783 to 1790, during those seven years, I continued to act, from principle and from passion, for a reform; not deeming that the duties of a good citizen, and a good physician, were at all incompatible; not believing that so liberal a procession should act in this country, as they might have been forced to have done at Rome, where they were chosen from the class and condition of slaves. Were the duties of the profession in all cases to obliterate those of the citizen, there could be no public, but at the moment of election; and however good the rule is, to mind our own business, there are times, when the business of the public is every man's own business, and the personal and general weal are the same.

On coming to this city, in the year 1790, I did not relinquish those principles, nor alter that mode of conduct, which I thought best suited the character of a good citizen. Sensible that Catholics and Protestants agreed in the essential articles of religious duty, and that though the form and ceremonial may vary, as the features of the face, the substance, like the construction of the heart, was, in all, alike; I co-operated in an union of sects, for the interest of the whole society, and against the dominancy, the political dominancy, of any religious persuasion. I believed the general character of mankind to be less influenced by the excellencies of religion, or injured by its abuses, than the mutual crimination of sects would lead us to imagine—a crimination often built on surmise and conjecture, or on a logic equally disgraceful. which builds the rule upon the exception, and poisons the judgment by pre-conceived impressions. I therefore entered into a society, of which this union of Catholic and Protestant Irishmen was the first stone and base, and a parliamentary reform the sole object and end. Nothing, surely, but the most intimate and heart-felt conviction of right intention, could have kept me attached to a society, which, during all its political life, has been the object of so much obloquy. Nothing could have supported me under the effects of professional injury, of the desertion of one valued friends, of being deemed as agent in the worst designs, and marked out by the eyes of those whom

I met in the streets, as a dark and malignant conspirator; nothing, I say, could have supported me, but that conscious mind, which is its own awful world; and which, I trust in God, will, at this hour, support me, even under the sentence of professional and personal ruin!

I thought it the duty of every good citizen who regarded the peace of Ireland, to cling to the people the more strongly, on the very account, that the panic of French principles and French practices, had made not only the upper ranks, but even the men of middling property, who had been accustomed to assimilate with the mass, now forsake and abandon the people, and the cause of the people—A PARLIAMENTARY REFORM. I thought it the very time for me to *popularize* themselves; and that it was most dangerous for men of rank, fortune, and connexions, to stand off, in sullen and suspicious sequestration, and thus make themselves be considered in no other light than as a political party, and a large predominating association, who have been so long accustomed to enjoy the whole constituent, as well as representative power, that their "scorn and horror" is readily excited at "the frenzy, folly, and wickedness" of those who desire any share in the legislation, or in the common rights of humanity. I did not think that it was the charity of individuals, or the munificence of the great, which could make the people happy, or keep them in peace. The social intercourse of the higher and lower orders ought not to be sustained solely by charity on the one hand, and blessings on the other, but by an adequate equivalent, given and received, that might make the poor and rich reciprocally *dependent*; and thus endowing every individual, however low, with an exchangeable value, must make the happiness of the community depend, not on inadequate and intermitting benevolence, but on the action and re-action of self-interest; a principle constant and universal. I thought (and acted from the thought) that the enjoyment of the elective right, could alone give this value to every man; and that, without it, there may be parties, and classes, and sects, and ascendancies—but there can be no people.

The great object of that society was, UNIVERSAL SUFFRAGE, and ANNUAL PARLIAMENTS; and their plan of reform was founded upon the eternal and immutable principle of justice. In repeating and justifying my political creed, I think I am defending myself from the imputation of sedition, by showing, as I can do, that none of these principles travel out of the constitution, but are justified by its philosophy, its practice, and the best authorities; and that all of these principles converge towards the permanent peace and happiness of my country—*for*, until there be an equality of rights, which it is the end of the social union to realize, and substantiate, there must be smothered *war* in civil society. I have appealed to the best constitutional *authorities*. "To be taxed without being represented," said Lord Chatham, with the energy of justice, "is contrary to the maxims of the law, and the first principles of the constitution." As all are taxed, all ought to be represented; and none can be represented, who has no power to vote. "Taxation and representation are inseparable," said Lord Camden. "In a free state," says Judge Blackstone, "every man who is a free agent, ought to be, in some measure, his own governor; and, therefore, a branch at least of the legislative power should reside *in the whole body of the people*." Thus, it is a vital *principle* of the constitution, that the property of the people cannot be granted, but by their own consent, in person, or by representative; and until the reign of Henry VI and the act of disfranchisement, which then dispossessed persons, and as it were appropriated the constitution, its PRACTICE also was built upon personal representation.

The British constitution is a conquest made, at different times, over the feudal system imposed by the first William; but the powers that made this conquest, were actuated by party interest, which accidentally, rather than intentionally, co-operated for the public good. The clergy and the barons combated and repressed the inordinate power of the monarch. But was it done for the good of the people? No! It was for the privileges of their noble rank, or for the safety of their sacred order. When commerce diffused property, a new resistance rose to the accumulation of power, made by the clerical and aristocratical factions. But was this resistance less selfish, though equally successful? No! The victories of these commons were the victories of sectaries, not of society; of parties, not of the people, of the proprietary interest, rather than of the general weal. Looking upward, the party is always for the people. Looking downward, they begin to vilify and abuse them. They are "the refuse and scum of the earth—mob—swine—sturdy beggars—of no value in the eye of God;" and any society who defends their cause is denominated "a blasted Jacobin society—wicked and vicious—the advocates of white-boys—scavengers, defenders, felons, paupers, and of Channel-row." The clergy maintained their order against the King: the nobles their rank against the clergy and King: the commons, their privileges against the clergy, nobles, and King: and the people are now to maintain their personal rights against the propertied and privileged community, including commons, clergy, nobles and King.

The *philosophy* of the constitution, which is nothing else than the improvement of human reason, concurs in proving that men alone can be represented, but not land nor money; that property does not confer any exclusive right to be represented; and that poor men, with an equal right, have more need to be represented than the rich. Those rights which the social union confirms and substantiates, are founded on *personality* alone; and since they are inherent in the nature of man, as man, they can never yield to, nor be extinguished by any acquired rights, such as property; which is a thing not natural, but incidental; which may or may not belong to a man; and which has no necessary connexion with either a good conscience, or a good understanding. When the right of property, which was comparatively late in its establishment, no longer confines itself to its own security, but lays a claim to dominion and ascendancy over the *anterior* rights of nature, converts persons into things and men into cattle; the intention of the social union seems to be defeated, and the land subjugates the inhabitants. Even on the supposition, that property is the rule of representation, the mass of property, the great fund of productive taxation, rests with the mass of the people; and though scattered into minute portions, is not less real, and ought to be as really represented as when cumulated in the hands of the comparative few.

"To give the mass of property, commercial and landed, the whole of the return of members to serve in parliament," is, in effect, to form the propertied community into one great corporation, whose end it may be, to league together, and combine their whole influence, against the population of the country; "a proprietary influence," which, however applauded, is, *at best*, but a conspiracy between two classes of people—the landholders and tenantry against the intendment of the constitution; a collusive traffic of franchise and private judgment, which the rich buy, and the poor sell. It appears to me, that the fluctuation which attends property is, of itself, a proof, how absurd it is to base the rights of man on a bottom so unstable; and still more so to draw circles around places, as if to encompass or confine a quality so fugitive, and to seat the genius of the constitution on the still revolving wheel of blind and capricious fortune; and hence, proceeding as far with a good principle as it would lead me, I thought it my duty, as a man, to advocate the equality of rights, a political equality, perfectly consistent with civil distinctions; and to reprobate any plan of reform which pets and cherishes portions of the community, to interest them in abuses; and to irritate the remainder by invidious comparison, which, by attaching the oldest inheritance of the *whole* people to certain round spots of earth, gives a locality to liberty, inconsistent with its nature: turns legislators into land-measurers, and land-measurers into legislators; extending lines of demarcation, on one side of which, privilege is heaped up, and on the other, common right trodden down: paling in with pieces of pack-thread, the liberality of the constitution, and circumscribing, with boroughmonger-authority, the principles of eternal justice.

The outline of my life, made up, as I presume to think, of pure intentions, and honest principles tending to maintain the rights of man, his dignity, his tranquillity, and his happiness, appears to me as a volume of circumstantial evidence against the charge, however positive, of having written or published a single paper with seditious intention; and in acknowledging, that as a citizen, I wish to strengthen the popular order of the government, the democratic or republican part of the constitution; actively persevering in a pursuit, which most of the choice and master spirits of the age have, I think, shamefully abandoned, seized with a panic that has congealed their principles; I do not think it any sign of sedition to have been proof against that panic—and to have felt the influence of what I should call a rational panic, a panic which leads me to dread the *Jacobite* more than the *Jacobin*, and the revival of those doctrines of passive obedience, non-resistance, and epidemic Toryism, which produced one revolution, and may provoke another. If *that* panic be not accounted seditious, which drives men, not only to abandon all exertions to rectify those abuses by which the constitution may have been perverted, but to countenance and connive at the violations it may have suffered, by their torpid acquiescence, passive concurrence, and strenuous inactivity; if *that* panic be founded on legal and constitutional principles, which has led these men to outrage the wretchedness of the people (who, though decried as dirt, are yet like the earth on which they tread, the great pabulum of luxury and enjoyment) by base allusions, and contumelious appellations, and by the low estimation thus set upon them, to sink them still lower in self-estimation, and drive them to abandonment and despair; is not *that* opposite panic as well founded, and as little allied to sedition, which makes me dread the effects of this terrible estrangement taking place between the upper and lower orders of society; which makes the wish of arbitrating and mediating between them, of averting their rude and revolutionary collision, by a reform of reason and accommodation; and of holding out that torch of instruction which may guide the infatuated rich, as well as the uninformed poor, in the just medium between their rights and their duties? Or is it to be construed into any intention of disturbing the public peace, if, on beholding the approaching extinction of an institution, which had raised this country from a state of brutal ferocity, and was advancing it to a perfect civilization, I should have addressed the Volunteers, in the fervour and in emphasis of the heart, and in terms, the mere shade or faint reflexion of what had been said by the most illustrious men? O memory of Grattan! let those words that made our hearts burn within us at the time, shield us now from the charge of sedition!

"The Irish constitution, commerce, and power, with you began, and with you they would vanish. You are the great charter of the nation, or efficient cause, and our final hope. Obnoxious for your virtue, you are to confirm your advocates, and to preserve your associations, the dreadful instrument of national deliverance. Believe me, you have many enemies; and you are to guard against false friends, and national foes; against the weakness of human nature, and the depravity of man, against sloth, against security, against administration, against a *militia*. I have heard your legality disputed. Conscious as I am that no law prohibits the subject to arm, convinced as I am, of your legality, I conceive that question to be lost in the immensity of your numbers; and with the pomp, and power, and trade, and all that train which await your progress, I shall not stop your army to ask what law has made you;—sufficient, that there is no law against you—sufficient, that without you, there could be neither law nor liberty! *Go on*, and prosper, thou sword of justice, and shield of Freedom—the living source of an ancient flame—the foundation of our pride—a providential interposition—an army, enriching the land with industry, costing the state nothing, adequate to all her enemies, and greater than all her revenues could pay. Awful! indeed, to the tyrant, but to the just prince unconquerable strength. The custody of the national's character is in your hands— Go on, and multiply, and add immortal security to the cause of your country."

Are not such awakening words hallowed in our remembrance? and is the faint echo of such sentiments to be now hallowed at as the rankest sedition? once rewarded with a popular pension, and now punished with fine and a prison? But the times are changed; alas! it is very true. Yet what are the times? The sun still makes the seasons, and the earth produces the harvest; but it is the change in *men's* dispositions which *unmake* the times, for truth is still the same, and rests on the base of its own immutability. Because men of station and abilities fell, at one time, into the ranks of the people, from mere panic, and in order to preserve their "proprietary influence;" and, at another time, from another panic, have forsaken that very institution which they had so warmly patronized, and reproach and vilify it for the very effects which their own abandonment had occasioned, was it sedition in a man to stand undisturbed by panic of the one kind, or panic of the other, on a firm and sound-set principle, that in an armed people lies the best security for public peace?— and does he deserve a jail for reverencing and thinking well of, and hoping much from the people in their lowest abasement—still recognizing in the tenant of the meanest hovel, the capability of human nature, and in the veriest wretch over whom he stumbles in the streets, deploring the victim of a corrupted public constitution?

With respect to this address to the Volunteers of Ireland, a paper raised from its intrinsic insignificance, *by serving as a plausible pretext for repeated prosecutions*, I do think there is an honest physiognomy, which indicates on its face the simple sincerity of the heart which dictated it. Let any man place himself, if he can, at an impartial distance from the paper, and he would characterize it as the hurried effusion of an enthusiastic mind, the general tenor of which was well-intentioned, but with some rash and imprudent expressions, probably arising from the difficulty of separating what was meant to be energetic, from what was really inflammatory; a composition which was easily pervertible to purposes unthought of by the author; a perversion which might be made by opposite parties, the one to obtain an instrument for sedition, the other to find a subject for prosecution; and thus the innocent author might become the dupe of inconsiderate friends, or the prey of watchful enemies. Though the paper may have been adjudged a libel, it may have been written without any libellous or seditious intention, and that may have been distributed with an intention of exciting commotion, which the writer certainly meant as a preservative of the public peace. The best intentions are liable to be abused; the best purposes perverted; and things written with the most pure and sincere heart, have been conjoined with the worst actions. Men have taken the Gospel in one hand, and the sword in another; and the word of the Scottish rebels, under Montrose, was, "*Jesus, and no quarter!*"

The subject matter of this prosecution is now a year and a half old. I will not presume to ascribe any improper designs in bringing it forward so long after the publication, and at this very invidious time, when plot and treason is so much talked of, that an innocent man may be prejudged, even by a supposed implication in crimes of which others have been accused; but if I, as the supposed author of this paper, had any designs of disturbing the public peace, it is strange, that they should not, in all this time, have manifested themselves in some other *overt acts*; that sedition did not go on into treason; and as there has been nothing of that kind produced by the ingenuity and vigilance of the crown lawyers, it is to me a strong presumptive proof, that I was as little seditious at the period of the publication, as I appear to have been both before and after it; and thus my whole life (a parte-post, as well as a parte-ante) seems to me a cumulation of evidence against the individual charge of sedition.

With respect to the informer in this prosecution, I can scarcely think it possible that conviction could be grounded on a *single* evidence, so notoriously influenced by a malicious mind, with vengeance on his tongue on all occasions, and virulence distilling from his pen, even *during* the pendency of the prosecution; but I have a pride in hating personalities; and leaving the commentary on such a character to others, I can only exclaim with Brasidas, when a rat seized him by the hand, that the most contemptible creatures acquire a portion of respect from their danger. "Although I have not the power to shake off the viper which comes out of the heat, and to remain free from harm," I am able, thank God so far to overcome an instinctive moral antipathy, as to acquiesce in the philosophical opinion, that such creatures, however odious to sense, are in the order of nature; and that there is a use in all things most venomous, though we are not able to find it out. But though I can view this being, swollen into dangerous significance, as a philosopher contemplates some reptile, magnified in the field of his microscope, yet I cannot help lamenting, that it should ever be necessary in any government, to foster a set of informers, and to place them, as Locusta was in the days of Tiberius, "inter instrumenta regni." I should have thought, that an argument very commonly adduced by modern as well as ancient Italian policy, would never have found an advocate in this land. "Egli è un huomo honesto, ma *'La Ragonia di Stato'* raichiede che sia punito."

My Lords, I have spoken with the assurance of innocence, and, I hope, without audacity. My defence rests on the *purity of motive*; and that purity may be deduced from the character of my conduct, and the consistency of my life. That little life has been rounded by a single benevolent principle, the object of which was to serve my country as far as *I* could serve her, in promoting a reform in parliament; and, as a means for this object, to elevate the public to a knowledge of their rights and their duties, and to perpetuate an institution which contributed to this high information. That the constitution was imperfect, as all the works of man are, it cannot be seditious to suppose; but that it can reform *itself*, or contains in *itself* a principle of rejuvenescence, I do not believe; or that those will ever contribute to its rectification, who are most interested in its abuses. The wish of every lover of peace, and his country, is not to rend, but to renovate; not to ruin, but to restore; not to anarchize, but to cement and consolidate—and that wish must look for its completion, not to this or that individual, not to a propertied community, not to a pusillanimous gentry, not to an interested opposition, not to a venal city, not to the rashness of a mob, but to the CONSTITUTIONAL INTERPOSITION OF THE WHOLE PEOPLE.

If I am to suffer, I hope to do it with patient equanimity; not the less sensibly feeling the horror of imprisonment, and the prospect of professional, and most probably personal ruin.

Dublin, 25th June, 1794.

[This DEFENCE was not delivered in Court, but (by advice) was communicated in such a way as to contribute to the acquittal which took place.]